?
AT if
_____
you can...

TO MIYA

DESIGN YOUR LIFE

VINCE FROST

LANTERN

an imprint of
PENGUIN BOOKS

DESIGNED AND PRODUCED IN AUSTRALIA

"All women, men and
All that we do, almost a
design is basic to all h
and patterning of any
foreseeable end consti
Any attempt to separ
thing-by-itself, works
design is the primary u

hildren are designers.
 the time, is design, for
manity. The planning
act toward a desired,
tes the design process.
e design, to make it a
ounter to the fact that
derlying matrix of life."

Victor Papanek, *Design For The Real World*, 1985

CONTENTS:

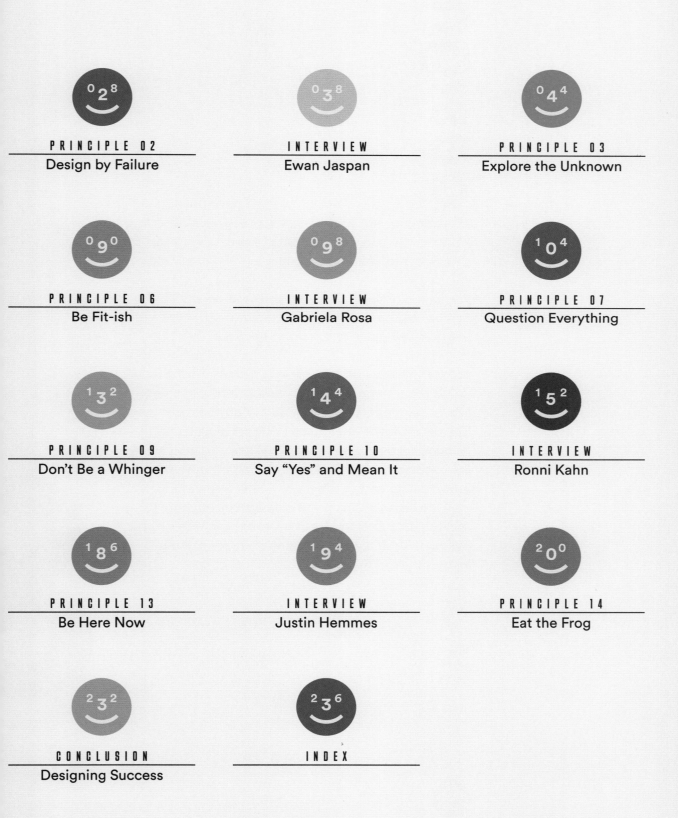

design:

has always been in my life. I have been designing for the past twenty-five years. I spend my working life helping other people solve their problems and design successful outcomes.

I've built a thriving practice, amassed an enviable number of accolades and earned the respect of my peers. By all measures, I am a success.

But for years my private life was a mess. Living life at full speed, I periodically reached rock bottom and felt like I was about to die. Mental and physical exhaustion would force me to stop and rest (which I hate). I'd become overwhelmed by the lack of balance and my unsustainable lifestyle. Overweight, overstressed, drinking and eating too much of the wrong foods, I fell into the depths of self-pity and panic, only to recharge insufficiently and head back into this battle against myself. I was designing and redesigning everything but myself.

I didn't have a moment of revelation but somewhere along the way I began to evolve. I can't say when it happened, but it seems I hired myself to help design a better life. I began applying principles from my work life to my personal life. And I found my flow: I am more reflective, more alive to my senses, more in touch with the people around me and more aware of my value. In short, I am happier.

This book is the next step in my evolution. If my design principles are valuable to me, perhaps they will be valuable to others. Or, more radically, help others to recognise their own value. By looking at the colourful and complicated landscape of my life and work, using my own wrong turns as points of reference, I hope to put each principle in context. Analysing the past is the easy part; it's designing the future that's hard. But it's never too late to start.

I have also included interviews with people who inspire me and whose insights have helped shape my approach to designing my life.

This book will not solve your problems. You have to do that yourself. And it will take lots of hard work. But I believe this book is more than words and images. It shows problems as opportunities, proves the impossible possible and hopefully, it will inspire you to work better at living better ● ● ●

I always **felt** inadequate. That something was missing.

ting

It took me a long time to see how the world worked – and I'm still learning now. I didn't do well at college; I had no idea what my options were for the future. Design school seemed like a last resort, so for want of other options I applied to the West Sussex College of Design and did a year's foundation course. ___That's when I got the tingling feeling. Design wasn't academic; sure, there were rules but they were more like boundaries on a field, a playground. ___I could use my intuition; I could be myself – who-ever that was. Suddenly, I was surrounded by a lot of other people who were like me. ___After that foundation year, I had to choose a discipline. For the first time in my life, I had options. But there was only one choice, and it wasn't mine to make. Graphics chose me. Every morning, I woke up with an adrenalin rush. I couldn't wait to go to college and get a brief – I wanted to be challenged.

The tingle became a hummmm.

ling

INFLUENCE

CAN

DAD MADE TYPE

We wouldn't be here today without our parents. That's a bit obvious, but my mother and father are a great influence on me. They were alternative, but conservative. Not hippies smoking pot. They didn't drop out of society, but they didn't accept the status quo. They questioned things. Back then, in the late 1960s and early 1970s, they were pioneers: they embraced vegetarianism, the utility and beauty of craftsmanship, of making things yourself, of collaborating with neighbours, acting locally. My parents are gentle creatures. They've been vegan for twenty years. They are mindful of not leaving a scar on the earth, of not hurting people or animals; they are concerned with wellbeing. My parents emigrated to Canada when I was six months old. Dad wanted to escape the English class system. Canada represented a world of opportunity. When I was five, he got a job at the *Vancouver Sun* newspaper, so I spent my formative years, aged five to sixteen, in White Rock, just south of Vancouver. Dad was a compositor – the person who sets the type for printing. He has a love of type, a love of words. He reads books voraciously, hundreds of them, across all subjects; his sole criteria is the quality of the writing and the strength of the ideas. Dad was always pointing out signs; I never even thought about why it was cool. Things are just there, around you. You don't know how they get there. Or that it's someone's job to create them. ___My dad was always bringing home type, and I started collecting letters. There was a wonderful publication around in those days, The Whole Earth Catalogue. It was something my dad had found: big, A3 and black and white. It influenced me at a profound level. I loved the smell, the weight of it and the size of it. Dad and I never spoke about it. But I was intrigued by it as a piece of design.

A VERY GRAPHIC COUNTRY

-VE OUT STANDING

Canada is a very graphic country. Canadian Indian art is incredibly well executed and consistent. We lived surrounded by the art of the Squamish nation. And then there was everything else. The hockey teams, the football teams, McDonald's, doodle-art, matchbox, hot rods, 7Eleven, Chevy. The shapes of the cars, demanding to be drawn. And nature. Trees, rocks and lakes. The silhouettes of the mountains looming over everything. Even the killer whales are iconic: black and white. I would make elaborate sketches of things, visual fantasies elaborating on what was already there. Always thinking: what else could this thing be? ___I was very shy. I wasn't very verbal or very present socially. I wanted to communicate but found it hard to break free from my persona – the quiet withdrawn kid. I was designing my life – but in a negative way.

___I often felt sorry for myself. I couldn't communicate how I felt. My thoughts were creating an outcome I didn't want. It's all about outcome – as I came to learn. It took a long time to gain confidence in my own opinions, to know what I liked and didn't like.

___When I visited my granddad – my father's father, Fred Frost – in England, he said: "Us Frosts, we know our place." A very English statement. It's all about not standing out. A lesson it took me a long time to unlearn. ___At the time I found England depressing, devoid of colour. The little houses all in rows. People wore grey. It didn't have the razzmatazz North America had. A can-do attitude. A bright positive outlook. England felt trapped, stuck in its ways. North America was the New World in every sense. Incredibly visual, a completely different energy and flow. In Canada we had a detached house, a double garage. It might have lacked the refinement and heritage of England, but we had space. We had colour. The suburbs were like a time-lapse picture – you'd pass a field one day and the next there'd be wooden frames and the next entire houses and then a subdivision. Houses were built in a matter of days, as if they'd come out of a cake-mix packet. Buy the land. Build a house. Seeing that happening all around, you see that design is more than just graphics. You could actually design your life.

○ ● ○ ○

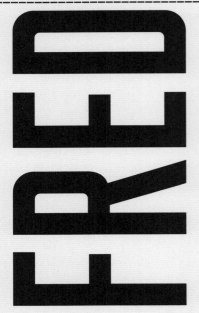

FRED

VACUUMING

————————————————Granddad was a lovely guy. After he retired from the military, he did a lot of painting, but I had no sense of the execution. The paintings were just there. His house was filled with them. He was always showing them to me, but to be honest I didn't connect with them, and I felt guilty about that. They needed context to make sense. A confession: to this day, the moment I get to a gallery I want to leave. Paintings should be a part of life. I don't like the way paintings feel hanging statically in a gallery. ___I was very good at not being present. I would go purple if I had to talk to a girl. It was horrific. I would go to a kid's birthday party and the next day at school the kid would say "Why didn't you come to my party?" And I had been there. I had made myself invisible. It's bizarre. I can do it today. If I don't feel comfortable in a meeting, I want to be invisible and start edging toward the exit.

————————————————————I was a neat freak. Fanatical about order. My room was immaculate. When I had any kind of chore, I would do it as quickly and accurately as I could. I wanted people to say "That was quick." "That was accurate." I cut lawns, washed neighbour's cars. I wanted it to be perfect. I would vacuum the grass. It was insane. The neighbour would say, "How did you do it so fast?" Mum would say, "You're back already?" It was a means of communicating. I didn't see it as a laborious chore. I did it in a way that gave me pride. I went above and beyond what most kids would do. ___I got a job at K-Mart. I wanted to stack the cans as perfectly as possible, label facing out. I wouldn't cut corners. Even on checkout, the other bag boys were telling me to slow down. I had the longest queue because the customers knew I was the fastest bagger. It wasn't showing off. My approach was, if you're do-ing the job, whatever it is, do it the best you can. ___I thought it was fun! ___Life was just getting inter-esting. Having a job, making money. Something other than school to get ready for. I liked looking at my little bank book and thinking "Wow, in a year I could have a thousand bucks!" Then, when I was fifteen my family moved back to England. What a shock. We were back in our place and we were expected to stay there.

OH MY GREEN GRASS

——————————————————————— At design school, I started to do well. It felt awful. My work stood out. I started to draw attention to myself. It was phenomenally uncomfortable. I did the work that created the praise but I didn't want the praise. I didn't feel as if I deserved it. It was complicated. ___I always felt – to the core of my being – it could be better. ___At art college, we all got the same brief and we'd go away to work on our ideas. At the time it was about the individual. Today it's more collaborative. Then, it was thirty people gathered around a table, and you would present your work. I dreaded that. I wasn't comfortable justifying what I did. I felt it spoke for itself. And that hasn't changed. I strongly believe our work should speak for itself. It shouldn't need explanation. ___The world of design was incredible at the time. We weren't taught about the history of design; you just had to look around: The Face, Harper's Bazaar, record albums, MTV. I started getting excited about editorial, storytelling, photography, art direction, looking at the people who were doing cool things and getting attention. ___My goal was to learn as fast as I could. I wanted to get the ideas out of my head as quickly as possible; out of my head and into the world. It was like cutting the grass back in White Rock: I could see in my head what it was going to look like, so I'd focus on making it happen. That kid in White Rock is still inside me, and I wrestle with him every day.

——————————————————————— When I was born, Dad told Mum that he wasn't going to let me be treated the way he was at home, school and work. He would see that I had a better life. That's why we went to Canada. Later he'd say, "I moved to Canada to give you a chance at something I never had. Go out and get it." It felt like a lot of responsibility. After all, "Us Frosts know our place." And I doubted myself. I wasn't the right man for the mission. I didn't have the outgoing personality that I associated with the go-getter. The man of action. My neighbourhood was filled with strong confident kids with strong confident parents who were good with words. Nothing stopped them; they had this phenomenal confidence. And I didn't.

SPLENDID

_____When I was ten years old, I stopped growing. There are pictures of me in school: I'm half the size of other kids. One day I was taking out my dirt bike when suddenly I felt really weak and I just fell off. My mum whisked me to the hospital. The specialists poked and prodded and scratched their heads. So they took me up to Vancouver General, in the children's ward with other kids my age, some of them dying of cancer. I was anaemic. I was weak. They probed some more. They cut me open, but they couldn't figure out what was wrong with me. I was in the hospital for a month, when finally they had their eureka moment. They discovered I had thirteen spleens, the result of a hyperactive growth hormone. Once those were removed, I started to grow. But I had been so weak and bedridden that I needed to learn to walk again. I missed a lot of school and when I went back I was behind. From that moment on I always felt as if I had to catch up, to prove myself to myself. Even today I don't feel I've caught up. I am still learning.

_____How well do you know yourself? I thought I knew myself. But I didn't have balance in my life. I spent years working like a dog. Design was the thing I put before everything else. Work was the most important thing. And the next most important thing was more work. Except that I didn't see it as work, I saw it as an opportunity. I was so excited. So hungry for opportunities, to do stuff, that I didn't want it to stop. Because I didn't want to fall behind. Not again. Not ever ●

OP-
PORT-
UNITY.

●○○○

The potential saving in time and energy in aligning yourself with someone who has got to where you want to be is invaluable. Think of it as leapfrogging through time. Look for someone you respect, someone who's a bit of a hero figure, and someone who inspires you and helps give clarity to complex situations. Having a range of accessible mentors can also be helpful — a wellbeing expert, a bank manager, a presentation coach, an accountant — having a diverse bunch of people creates a support mechanism and protects you from making mistakes.

frog
p

0 1 7

I NEEDED A MENTOR

I DIDN'T KNOW I NEEDED A MENTOR

I graduated from design school in 1983. I needed a job, and I had a few different ones before I found a home at Pentagram, the design firm. I needed a mentor. I didn't know it, but I instinctively sought one. There were two men at Pentagram who stood out for me, Alan and Ken. They weren't officially mentors, but I admired them and felt inspired by them. The kid from White Rock was watching, observing how they worked, how they dressed, how they conducted themselves in meetings. Even their physical gestures: if they smoked, how did they smoke? I was so in awe of them, I was nervous about communicating with them. ___Alan Fletcher was in his 70s. His clothes were from the 70s: denim vest and slightly flared jeans; he was always in jeans. The creases were like knife-edges. His wife must have ironed them. His glasses were always at the end of his nose. A chain smoker – they smoked in the studio back then. Gruff. Eastender. Bloody smart. A creature from the days when everything was handmade, hand-drawn. He was phenomenally neat. He collected graphic accidents: crushed Coke cans arranged on his pinboard. He has written some beautiful, highly regarded books. I first encountered him through his work: warm and friendly and smart and funny. But as a person he seemed unapproachable. He was the opposite of what his work was like. ___Kenneth Grange was slightly older than Alan. And seemed much crankier. He designed Kodak cameras and kettles, like the Marc Newson of his time. ___Pentagram had an open-plan studio. I was there working late one night; so late it was early morning.

SHADOW A STAR

018

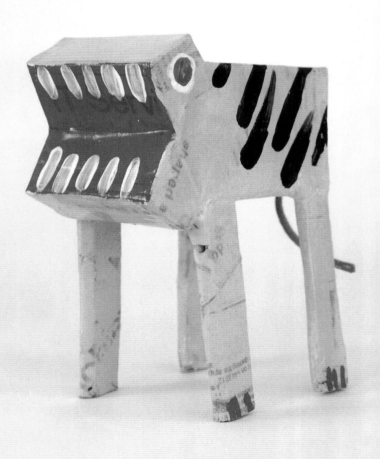

Hooligan by Alan Fletcher
Courtesy of Paola and Raffaella Fletcher

"I find going to bed and pulling my imagination over my head often means waking up with a solution to a design problem. The time between sleeping and waking seems to allow ideas to somehow outflank the sentinels of common sense. That's when they can float to the surface." – Alan Fletcher

Ken had a nook in the studio with a treasured posses-sion: a beautiful Eames Chaise lounge. I was tired; it was 4 a.m., so I thought I'd lie down for a minute. And I fell asleep in the Eames. I was woken up by a very angry bear. "What the fuck are you doing in my chair?" They were the first words he said to me. I was Goldi-locks. I legged it out of there. I learned that however much you admire someone, everyone has boundaries. They're only human. Sometimes you only learn where those boundaries are by stepping over them. ___One day, Alan said, "Come round my house and we'll have a glass of wine and talk about your future." I was so excited. He had this fantastic house in Pembroke Mews in London. He poured me the promised glass of wine and we sat there looking at each other. Two weirdos. Finally, he asked, "Do you want to be famous? Or do you want to be rich?" I said I wanted to be famous, like him. I'm not sure that was the answer he was looking for. But it was true. ___Looking back on my time at Pentagram, I learned a bit about design, but I didn't learn anything about running a business. When I left to start my own business, I got a nice-ish office. I got a computer. I got a phone. And I sat there. OK, now what? Of course, no one knew I was avail-able. I didn't have a clue. That was phenomenally naïve. But if I hadn't been so naïve, I might not have left. I might still be there. Perhaps that would have been more naïve; it's hard to know. ___Later on I realised – and it took me a long time – that it's okay not to be good at everything, to admit your weak-nesses. That it's okay to ask for help. It took quite a bit of reprogramming; I was very resistant, but it's been worth it. Since then I've found a variety of mentors for myself: clients who've become friends, financiers, my naturopath – all experts in their own fields who can help guide me. Some I just catch up with informally; others I'll book a Skype session with and discuss different approaches to specific issues in my business. Mentors come in all shapes and sizes; some won't even know the influence they've had on your life, while you can set up a more formal relationship with others. Learn from everyone you can ●

THE F#%K ARE YOU

IN MY CHAIR?"

Eames Chaise lounge, designed by Charles and Ray Eames

PRINCIPLE 01

work out what you need help with and then find the best person to guide you

learn

you might learn from mistakes but it's better to avoid them altogether

avoid

stakes

"Try Again. Fail again. Fail better."Samuel Beckett
Design is a process of internal failure. When you're working on a brief, you try out lots of ideas. Mock them up, play with what they look like. Try prototypes until you get one that sticks. Design by failure. Saying that, I don't believe in failure. Failure for me is giving up. Don't give up. Focus on constantly tweaking and improving your ideas. Don't expect your ideas to be perfect from the beginning. Perfection can be intimidating and it can stop you in your tracks, which happens to me a lot. Just start — get your idea down, try it, live with it, tweak it — you can always come back to it or let it go. If it's a mistake, learn from it. In business and in life, nothing is fixed so have the agility to evolve with the times and the determination to keep trying.

don't giv

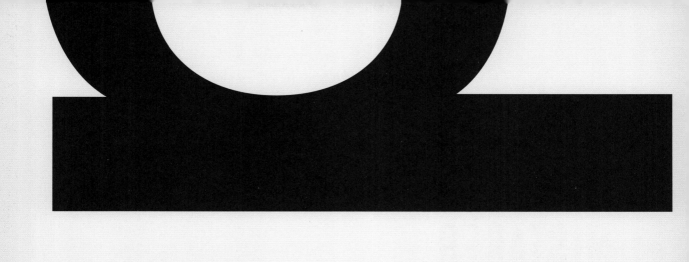

IT'S THROUGH MISTAKES THAT YOU ACTUALLY CAN GROW YOU HAVE TO GET BAD IN ORDER TO GET GOOD

Paula Scher, Designer

When I left Pentagram and set up my own studio, I sat there waiting for the world to come to me. And nothing happened. I started to beat the bushes. I got out of the studio. No more hiding in plain sight; I had to make a living. You put stuff out there and the more you do, the more it attracts back to you. But there wasn't just designing to do. All the details, big and small, the moving parts that were invisible to me at Pentagram, needed doing. I tried to control every single element in the business and in my life, and the speed got to the point where I couldn't manage it. ___Having my very first assistant was phenomenally hard. It was hard to work with this guy. He wasn't me! I needed the help but I didn't know what to do with it. I made him cry several times, and ended up doing two people's work. Then I resented him even more because I was paying him. I had the ideas in my head, but this ninny couldn't read my mind! When I left him alone, he didn't do the things that I would have done. It's hard to delegate that work. It's hard to bypass that process that you've used year after year. So I got my next assistant, and the next one and the next one. And I was still the busiest person in the business. ___The work was going out. The world was coming to me. I was asked to judge global design competitions, asked to contribute articles to design publications. And I did. And that took even more time. I was flattered. But every assignment, every brief that came in put the onus on me: ___"I owe them the best job possible." ___If I had known then what I know now: my first assistants were paralysed by my lack of trust. So they didn't trust themselves to do anything, lest they upset me. The only thing they did that I would have done is leave. I found more victims. Soon I had a studio with five people. Which meant more work for me. I worked my brains out. I was so focused on the design projects in front of me, I couldn't deal with the "business" of design. I didn't know how to delegate. My left and right brain didn't function as one.

I NEED A HAND BUT I DON'T KNOW WHAT TO DO WITH IT

___By 1995, I had moved into a great studio space on Great Sutton Street in Clerkenwell. I had a staff of six. Six people reporting to me. I was excited, frustrated, exhausted, stretched. And they were asking things from me that I didn't know how to resolve. You get so busy that someone's been working for you for three years and you barely know them. They get unhappy and they leave. And you curse yourself: why didn't I look after that person? Why didn't I understand their ambitions, accommodate them, nurture them? I had failed them. ___"It's through mistakes that you actually can grow. You have to get bad in order to get good.' Paula Scher ___I came to realise – through a lot of pain and stress and uncertainty (trying and failing) – that I had to be a manager. That it was a separate task in itself and I needed to delegate a part of myself to the process. I didn't trust that part of myself but I had

Hand Made my hands photographed by Giles Revell in his studio in Clerkenwell. For the cover of *Wallpaper** magazine 2012

EVOLVE YOURSELF TO

work
ing

INSTEAD OF

work

no choice. Michael Gerber says "You have to delegate, not abdicate." You need to be clear about your vision for the business and make sure the people who work for you understand that vision. When you work out how to do that, you realise how valuable your people are. It was only when I learned to enjoy being a manager, to make sure I had the right people and to trust them that things really began to improve.
___Most businesses are started by someone who is good at something, a technician. But they have no idea how to run a business. They know how to do what they do but they don't know how to make the business succeed. And that's why most new businesses fail. Because they have no vision, or if they do, no systems in place to support it. ___"Most entrepreneurs are merely technicians with an entrepreneurial seizure. Most entrepreneurs fail because you are working IN your business rather than ON your business. Michael Gerber ___The only reason my business didn't fail is because I spent the better part of ten years at a fever pitch. Externally, everything looked great. Good clients. Good projects. Good staff. The work was getting done. Somehow I got married, had a kid. And it's all a blur. Until Japan ●

(in)g
YOUR BUSINESS

"It is very importar
and to do a lot of st
possible — with as li
It's much, much be
a lot of crap having
think in the begin

to embrace failure

f — as much stuff as

e FEAR as possible.

er to wind up with

ried it than to over

ng and not do it."

Stefan Sagmeister, Designer

TRY
AGAIN
FAIL

0 3 6

Samuel Beckett

AGAIN. FAIL. BETTER.

Relentless

Ewan Jaspan is Australia's highest ranking kiteboarder.

Ewan Jaspan

INTERVIEW 01:

What really motivates you to do what you do? How did you discover kiteboarding?

My whole life I've been interested in kites; before I can even really remember my parents were flying kites on the beach; I just had a fascination with them. When we moved to Australia, we moved to St Kilda right on the beach, and I really wanted to give it a go. I pretty much got hooked on it straight away, and it kind of took over. It really became my life; that's my job now. My love for it motivates me, and the more I learn, it keeps me hooked, and I want to get better and travel, see more places, meet new people and all that.

You've found something that you absolutely love doing that you can also get paid to do. Is it difficult at times, or does it just come naturally?

For the first couple of years I wasn't taking it super seriously, because I'd just gotten into it, just as a sport to do. And so I did that for a while and then kind of got to the top and realised I needed to do a lot more work. Suddenly it was my job where I've got to take it a lot more seriously and keep myself fit, train, and not do anything stupid, and try to prevent injury as much as I can.

Do you ever feel like giving up?

No, I haven't ever thought about giving it up. I'm recovering from a shoulder injury at the moment but I'm still definitely in love with the sport, and I want to know that I've given it a good shot before I think about giving it up. I still feel I'm yet to reach my potential, and can still work a lot harder, and experience a lot more. The injury's set me back; it's hard to get motivated sometimes. I've only just in the last week or two been able to go to the gym and start doing stuff again; I've been pretty immobilised, and it does get to you; it's such a difference from what I'm used to, so it gets you down a bit. But if anything it's motivating me more now to get back on the water and do better.

How much of it is about you doing it because you love it, and how much of it is motivated by your competitive spirit of wanting to win?

I kind of want to see myself in both sides of the sport. I enjoy making videos and free riding and those kinds of more social events, and going to great spots with friends and discovering new places, but it's not so much where the money is at the moment, and where you can make a name for yourself; that's still in the competitive side. I think I've got more to offer the sport in terms of videos and just doing something a little bit different from everyone else. But I think it's the same with anyone, the better you do in competitions, the more you love them and the more you enjoy them. But I always do kiteboarding for myself, I'm not really doing it for anyone else; I do it for my sponsors and that, but I wouldn't be doing it if I wasn't enjoying it.

Ewan in the air at the PKRA event in Pingtan, China, November 2013

And is it a solo thing – is it you and the kite and the board and that's it, or is there a team behind you?
It's not really a team sport. All the heats are one on one. But it's a very social sport; because it's quite solo on the water, everyone chats when they're off. In Melbourne for example there's a huge community of kiteboarders, and everyone's really good friends and catches up outside, not just at the beach, they catch up all the time outside the sport, and there's a big social scene, which is great. It's a very friendly sport; everyone wants to help each other out. Off the water everyone wants to chat about their session or some new trick they just went out there and tried, things like that.

What does it feel like to win?
It's great. It's probably the best part of the sport when you stand up on the podium at the end and everyone's cheering. It's what I always wanted to do, win competitions and do well, and put myself up there, and when you do it, it's nice to see that it's all paying off.

And then, equally, what does it feel like to lose? Or rather, to be further down the ranking?
It depends on your goals; what winning and losing is for you. When I was on a world tour last year and I got 5th place, that was a huge win for me, because I'd finished last year at 20th or something, so it felt like winning to me. It doesn't feel great going from my best result to not a great one, but you have to work hard to make sure you're not demotivated by it or you're never going to really get better.

So how do you pick yourself up out of that?
Even simple things like having a really good session, or landing on your trick, picks you up. You can go out one day, just ride really well and in a training session as well just land all the tricks you want to, and you feel like "Wow, if I can do these tricks in a competition, there's no reason I couldn't win." Every time you improve, it picks you out of that slump, and you feel better about yourself. You've got to switch that side of your brain off that's saying "I'm not going too well."

Do you have a coach that helps you?
No, I don't. In kiteboarding people have fitness coaches and that kind of stuff, but they don't have someone that trains them specifically towards a trick. The best way to progress is going places for training and focusing, watching people, riding with people who are at your level or better than you, constantly pushing you. Like all the time I spent riding with Alex Pastor, who's the world champion, he's from Spain. Just watching him do tricks that I can't do, it's like "I really want to do that, I want to learn this", and then you chat to him about it, and he'll say "Try this, this is how you do it", and then you go out and try it, and you get closer. There's a lot of figuring stuff out for yourself, trying and failing and finally getting it.

It must take a lot of relentless pursuit to get it right.
You can never do every trick in the book, but there's always something you can add. You never reach the limit, there's always more to do, so it keeps you motivated.

You've reached an unusually high level; why do you think that is?
I think living close to the beach helped me; I was on the water every time it was windy, longer than anyone else, until dark nearly every night. Mum would have to drag me in to do my homework and have dinner!

Did it cause problems with your school?
Yeah, it did a bit. It was all I wanted to do and it was hard to think "Oh, but I've still got to do school." But I still did well at school; I got into the uni course that I wanted to get into.

What would you do if you didn't do kiteboarding?
Probably what all my other mates at school are doing, maybe taking a gap year and travelling a bit; I wouldn't have gone straight into university. I think I'd still be riding back in Melbourne, then going to university and just hanging out with mates and maybe doing a bit of travelling. But I don't really see myself being able to just sit in one place doing university and going partying every weekend, it's not really what I want to do.

As an athlete, I guess you've got to look after your wellbeing as well – not party too hard?
Yes, but even if I wasn't, it doesn't really interest me that much, going out and clubbing and stuff. People invite me and I think, oh, I could do that, or I could get up tomorrow morning and feel good and then go do something.

What does it feel like to be in the zone?
When you're in the zone and you're landing everything, it's such a good feeling. Nothing distracts you; everything is focused on landing tricks and just doing your best, and that's when you win competitions or do well or land new tricks. Then you'll come in and you'll be all buzzing, you'll be like "That was amazing, that was such good fun, I did this, I worked that," or "I beat this guy and I'm just stoked by it."

How much fear is involved?
If you've got really strong winds, it gets quite dangerous, so I feel that fear sometimes. And sometimes you do a really big jump and your stomach drops, and you go "Wow, I'm really high up," like 20, 30 metres in the air. One of my favourite spots to do big jumps in high winds is down at Brighton, because you're inside this marina, and when you jump 30 metres in the air, you can see Brighton and Sandringham and half of the city. I've done that so many times now that it's not really scary. But every now and then you get a a big gust of wind and you go that bit higher, and you kind of shit yourself.

How much do you think you're affected by positive and negative mindsets?
Often the heats I do best in are when I'm against someone who's better than me, because there's no shame in losing, when you're against the world champion or something, and you just go out and you think "All right, I'm going to get real focused on this and just do my best, and it doesn't matter what happens." But if I'm against someone I should be beating, then I'll actually get a bit nervous, like "If I lose this, it's not going to look good." Then I try and play it a bit safe, and that's when you start knowing that you're not in the zone, you're not focusing properly; it's not working for you, and then you try and change it up and that doesn't work. But the judging criteria is based on how fast you go and how high you go and how technical you are, so really you've got to put everything into every trick, otherwise you're not going to win. So when you start playing it safe because you're a bit scared, it doesn't pay off.

Is kiteboarding your whole life? Is there much room in your life for anything else?
Well, right now, yes, there is room because I'm injured. And I really enjoy travelling. I have time to go see other places, and just travel with mates, and I've got a girlfriend who I've been with for a while now. I get to see her quite a bit, and she'll come travel with me sometimes. She's at university at the moment, here in Melbourne. But there's not really much time for anything like a university degree or a job as well.

What's does "design your life" mean to you?
Basically I'd say just to do what you want to do. In my case, I wanted to kiteboard, and I've spent the last few years building my life around that, and making that what my life is. You do whatever it takes ●

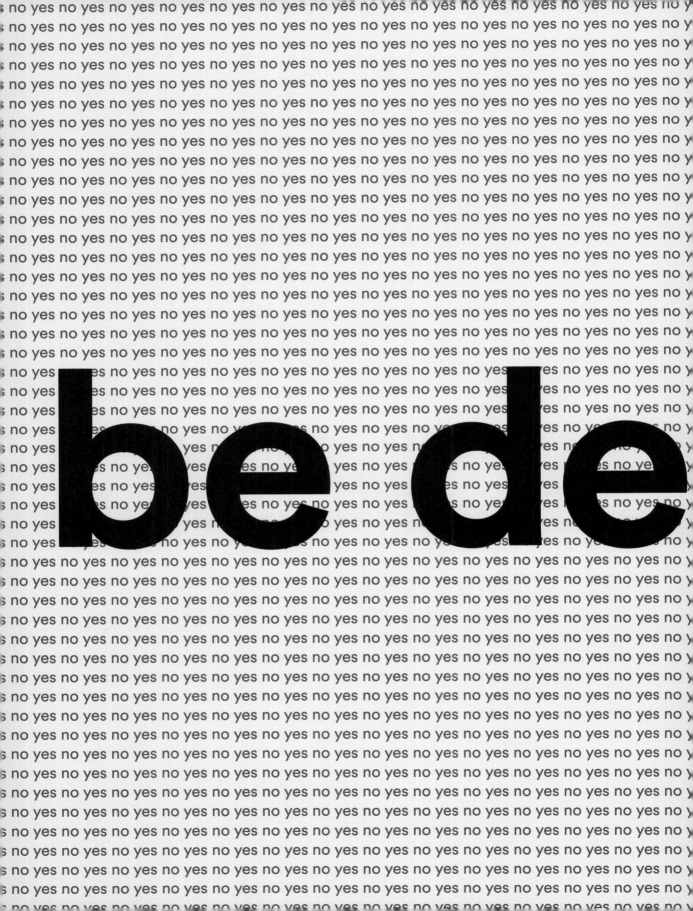

yes no yes no yes no yes no yes no yes no yes no yes no yes no yes no yes no yes no yes no yes
yes no yes no yes no yes no yes no yes no yes no yes no yes no yes no yes no yes no yes no yes
yes no yes no yes no yes no yes no yes no yes no yes no yes no yes no yes no yes no yes no yes
yes no yes no yes no yes no yes no yes no yes no yes no yes no yes no yes no yes no yes no yes
yes no yes no yes no yes no yes no yes no yes no yes no yes no yes no yes no yes no yes no yes
yes no yes no yes no yes no yes no yes no yes no yes no yes no yes no yes no yes no yes no yes
yes no yes no yes no yes no yes no yes no yes no yes no yes no yes no yes no yes no yes no yes
yes no yes no yes no yes no yes no yes no yes no yes no yes no yes no yes no yes no yes no yes
yes no yes no yes no yes no yes no yes no yes no yes no yes no yes no yes no yes no yes no yes
yes no yes no yes no yes no yes no yes no yes no yes no yes no yes no yes no yes no yes no yes
yes no yes no yes no yes no yes no yes no yes no yes no yes no yes no yes no yes no yes no yes
yes no yes no yes no yes no yes no yes no yes no yes no yes no yes no yes no yes no yes no yes
yes no yes no yes no yes no yes no yes no yes no yes no yes no yes no yes no yes no yes no yes
yes no yes no yes no yes no yes no yes no yes no yes no yes no yes no yes no yes no yes no yes
yes no yes no yes no yes no yes no yes no yes no yes no yes no yes no yes no yes no yes no yes
yes no yes no yes no yes no yes no yes no yes no yes no yes no yes no yes no yes no yes no yes
yes no yes no yes no yes no yes no yes no yes no yes no yes no yes no yes no yes no yes no yes

cisive

yes no yes no yes no yes no yes no yes no yes no yes no yes no yes no yes no yes no yes no yes
yes no yes no yes no yes no yes no yes no yes no yes no yes no yes no yes no yes no yes no yes
yes no yes no yes no yes no yes no yes no yes no yes no yes no yes no yes no yes no yes no yes
yes no yes no yes no yes no yes no yes no yes no yes no yes no yes no yes no yes no yes no yes
yes no yes no yes no yes no yes no yes no yes no yes no yes no yes no yes no yes no yes no yes
yes no yes no yes no yes no yes no yes no yes no yes no yes no yes no yes no yes no yes no yes
yes no yes no yes no yes no yes no yes no yes no yes no yes no yes no yes no yes no yes no yes
yes no yes no yes no yes no yes no yes no yes no yes no yes no yes no yes no yes no yes no yes
yes no yes no yes no yes no yes no yes no yes no yes no yes no yes no yes no yes no yes no yes
yes no yes no yes no yes no yes no yes no yes no yes no yes no yes no yes no yes no yes no yes
yes no yes no yes no yes no yes no yes no yes no yes no yes no yes no yes no yes no yes no yes
yes no yes no yes no yes no yes no yes no yes no yes no yes no yes no yes no yes no yes no yes
yes no yes no yes no yes no yes no yes no yes no yes no yes no yes no yes no yes no yes no yes
yes no yes no yes no yes no yes no yes no yes no yes no yes no yes no yes no yes no yes no yes

Comfort comes from the Latin "to strengthen". When we think of a comfort zone, we think of the status quo, of a slackened mental state. When you're in your comfort zone you don't need to be on your toes. But seen from another perspective, our comfort zone is the place that gives us strength so that we can move outside of that zone. A home is not merely a refuge, a place to escape, but also a place to recharge. Each day has its natural challenges. Challenges that you cannot predict. You have to step outside your comfort zone. Expand your consciousness. Whether it's your career or your life, it's how you grow.

I FELL IN LOVE WITH THE PEOPLE AND THE CULTURE BUT THE JOB KILLED ME.

As a kid, any new social situation was incredibly uncomfortable. When I started at Pentagram, and again when I started my own design firm, I was nervous but I knew in my heart I had to do it to come out stronger. And it didn't take long to feel confident. I still have moments of insecurity in creative situations. Any designer does. But you learn that creativity is a muscle strengthened by practice. Any new job, no matter how complicated, is exhilarating. You look back, thinking: "We didn't think we were going to make it. We pushed ourselves and we made it." But every now and again life serves you a Japan. ___Moving to Japan was a disaster. It was a great example of how not to design your life. It gave me exposure to a phenomenal country; I fell in love with the people and the culture but the job killed me. I was somebody's good idea, and it all went sideways. ___It was 1997. London was the coolest city on the planet. It was the days of Cool Britannia and I had a reputation as a magazine designer. This was a misplaced notion; I had designed a few magazines but had never done the full in-house gig. Condé Nast was launching Vogue Japan and Vogue Russia. Jonathan Newhouse, the Chairman and Chief Executive, was living in London and his wife, Ronnie, recommended me for the position of Art Director. In fact, they gave me the choice of Tokyo or Moscow. I chose Tokyo. ___First-class Heathrow to Narita. An apartment in Shoto Shibuya. It was incredible. I was like the kid in White Rock all over again. The colours, the sounds, the signs, the craftsmanship. Just buying a pen in a store – the careful folding of paper around the purchase – was an aesthetic experience. Tokyo blew me away. ___My thing was designing headlines. In English. Playing with the meaning of the words, not just the shape of the text. Japanese was exactly the wrong palette. The characters are entirely different, the sentences travel down the page, and pages flip to the left. I usually treat words with such respect, but Japanese became blurb. I was lost.

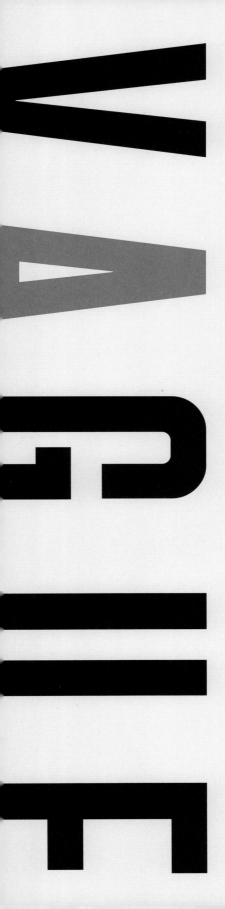

___I had a brainwave. I had to learn fast. I know, I thought, I'll bring in the best photographers and designers in Japan and get them to help me. But I learned too late it doesn't work like that. There was the small matter of etiquette. I asked the photo editors to send me the portfolios of the top Japanese photographers. Standard operating procedure: you want to know what's out there. ___Not in Japan. In Japan, an art director doesn't ask for portfolios without first committing to the photographer. So all these photographers, the crème de la crème, were telling everybody that they were working for Vogue Japan. I managed to piss off every major photographer in Japan. It was a PR disaster. ___It got worse. I went out on a few shoots. The photographers behave differently; it's much more hierarchical. My presence compelled them to show me every shot. I didn't want to interfere. I was waiting for the translator to finish and then waiting for the response in Japanese and then the translation into English. I felt like a fraud. I wasn't outside my comfort zone. I didn't have a comfort zone. ___I went to some local design schools, thinking I'd find some interns, some young guys, just like I would have done in London. But this was Japan. They didn't do internships. One young fellow came to interview for a position as a lay-out artist. He pulled open his portfolio and showed me painting after painting. I said, through the translator, "You do know we're looking for a layout person." The translation came back: "I am a painter." I didn't know how to respond to this. So I asked, "Why would you want to work at Vogue?" He answered, "I imagined it would be so uncomfortable that it would help me with my art." I didn't hire the guy, but the comment stayed with me. There's stretching your comfort zone, and then there's being in the wrong zone altogether. ___Japan was messing with me: just getting to work was devastating, the subway was incomprehensible. I went out to buy milk for my six-month old son and came back with lemon milk. My then wife was climbing the walls. No comfort zone.

___Finally after eight months, the publisher came into my office. "Things aren't working out." It was an eloquent understatement. I hadn't failed better. I had failed spectacularly. The editor and I were fired. It would have been harder for the editor. He was Japanese. He had to live there. I could go back to London with valuable lessons learnt, where the studio and the rest of my life were waiting. Who knows what would have happened if I had chosen Moscow?

___Now I'd say: do things that stretch you, to be sure, but be very thorough about investigating what the job is going to involve. Get a lawyer to go over your contract; get your objectives clear and don't be distracted. Japan was excruciating, but it's probably saved me from other, much worse mistakes ⬢

grov

stretching yourself beyond your comfort zone will grow your mind

"If someone offe
opportunity and you'r

say yes - then lear

you an amazing

not sure you can do it,

how to do it later"

Richard Branson

NE
IFORT
E

it will take you to exciting new places

know your

push but don't break yourself

limits

Be

A Z X
F C Y
C K H
T L S
O Z
U G
G H L
Z T
R J K
I C H
T Z Y
Z R F

life is far more interesting when you are challenged

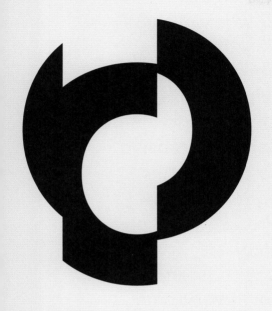

once you've made a decision, don't chop and change

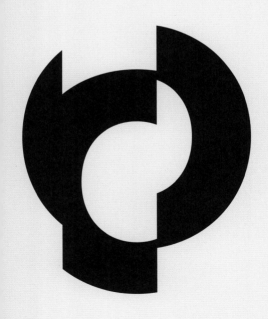
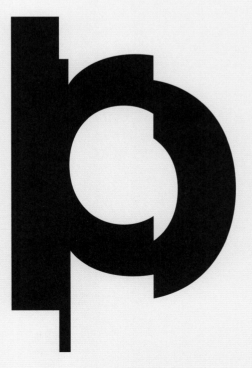

It's important to not stop seeing. As we get older, we think we know how everything works and we stop seeing the things around us. In a child's eyes, everything is new, fresh and exciting. Free from the restraints of convention. They create stuff by getting in there, making a mess, playing around and going crazy. They bring ideas to life in a spontaneous way – a lighthearted not labour-intensive approach. They have fun. I urge you to go back to the playground, unlearn all the school rules, get rid of any preconceived ideas of how you think you're going to solve a problem (because problems, like design briefs, are never straightforward) and look at things with fresh eyes. Find your spirit. Remember, you don't know everything. Not at twenty, not at fifty.

k i : t i r i

sp : : sp ds

A KID REPRESENTS THE NEW OPTIMISM HAPPINESS, NAIVETÉ

Back in London, post-Tokyo, I took some very deep breaths. It's good practice for when you have children. My son, Luca (the lemon milk baby) was born in 1997. Louie came in late 1999. My daughter Gia arrived in 2003. I struggled to balance my family commitments with running a new business. I needed to work to support my family, but the demands of the business made it hard to spend time with them during the week. I was drowning in it until I started to take time out. ___A kid represents the new. Optimism. Happiness. Naiveté. Eyes wide open. Questioning. Trying. Learning. Exploration is innate. Opening and closing cupboard doors. Sometimes they pinch their fingers. When I watched my kids making mess, taking pleasure in putting paint everywhere, putting colours down, it gave me pleasure. It's fascinating to see how they hold materials, the effort they put into it, spontaneous and quick. "Bang, I've done it." You don't have to tell them what to draw. There's a lot to be learned from that. Kids are naturally creative, naturally expressive. They are not conscious of history. They are in the moment, in the now. As kids get older we tell them what to draw. When you go into a school and see the artwork on the walls, in the early years you see those wonderful abstractions and then over time they devolve into clichés of houses, family and cars. ___My uncle Rod emigrated to Canada at around the same time as my parents. He's an artist in the purest sense. He lives it. He worked with native craftspeople, learned their techniques. He makes whirligigs and totem poles. When I was around eight, he came across Canada from Toronto to see us in Vancouver. He had a station wagon with these long poles poking out the back. ___Me: "What's that?" ___Uncle Rod: "It's my teepee."___We went camping in his teepee. At the entrance to the provincial park, there was a list of user fees: this much for a tent, this much for a trailer, this much for a Winnebago. Uncle Rod said: "Whattaya charge for teepees?" We were ducking under the windows, dying of embarrassment. We were kids acting like adults. Uncle Rod never stopped being a kid.

Uncle Rod, Rachel, Daniel, Naomi and me in his teepee. White Rock, BC

Luca and Louie Frost at bathtime 2002

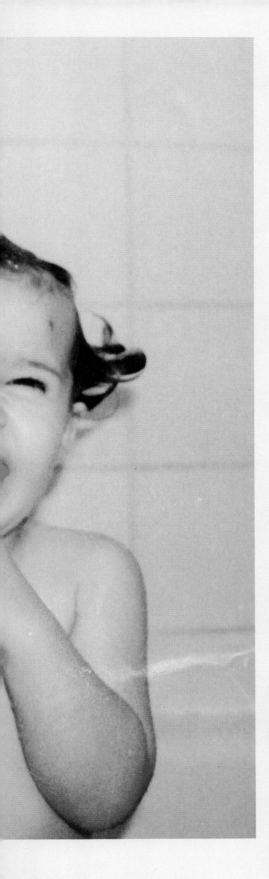

As a designer you have a brief window to create an impression. People are going to work, passing a poster or a bus. When you're taking things in for the first time going down Oxford Street – whether your Oxford Street is in Sydney or London or Tokyo – there's a massive three-dimensional quilted collage of information demanding attention. But after you've gone down that road twice a day for a couple of weeks, the mind is only going to spot something new. The rest is background. You need something that stands out.
___How do you design a book that will sit in a bookshop with 1000 other books all saying, "Look at me"? How does a café stick out on a streetscape? That's the challenge: How do I take a brief in print and create an emotion? You have to look at it with fresh eyes. You have to think of that strip as a playground. You have to have fun, remind yourself that you don't know everything. However old you are. ___Never stop being a kid. Never stop growing up. But stop being a teenager – it's a very unreasonable stage of life. And banish the phrase, "whatever" from your vocabulary ●

The many faces of Louie Frost

"I prefer comir
as little knowled

trying to lo
CHILDLE

to a field with

e as possible and

k at it with

KE eyes."

Tom Dixon, Industrial Designer

I find that the more positive my outlook, the more good things happen

bring love to life

don't worry about being neat and tidy, express yourself openly and without caution

Ru

new ideas can come from breaking old rules

Okay, so this isn't strictly a design "principle". It's about home, which for me, is an essential part of designing your life. Your home is a blank canvas. It's practical as well as a sanctuary. Get the basics that will give you comfort in your own home. Get a great bed. Introduce light and the smells you like. Use colours that bring you calm or joy. And moving house – great! Moving is growing. A chance to do it all over again, but make it better. To get rid of the stuff that makes you feel heavy. To take stock and live lighter.

Designing is about redesigning.

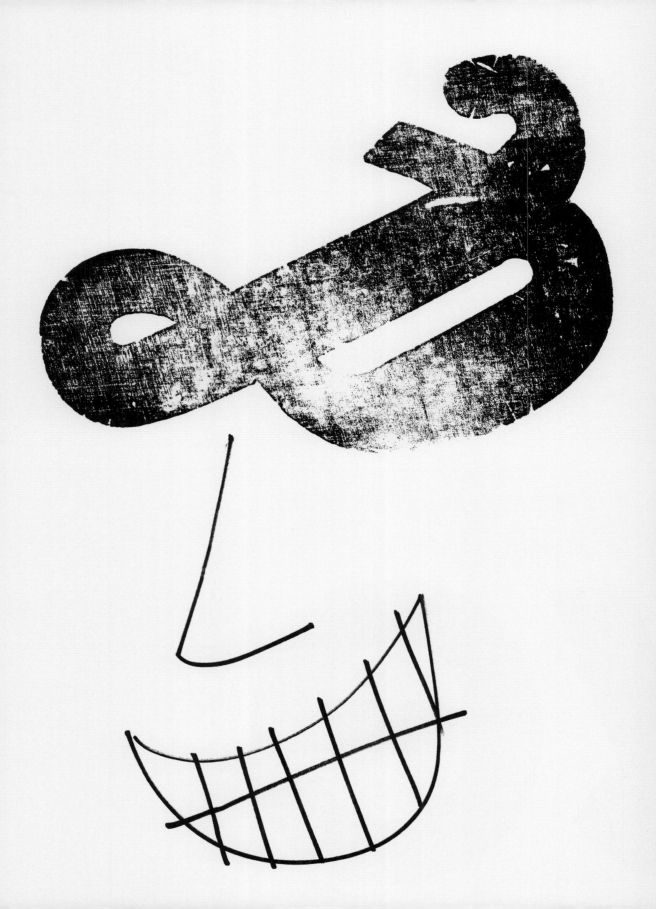

I was designing my surroundings from an early age.
If I had coloured walls I would paint them white.
I loved the change in the light. The blank slate. A
starting point. The chance to design a space around
yourself, an environment that creates a positive
reaction in you. ___And then I moved. And moved
again. I was a nomad. They say moving is one of the
most stressful things you can do. I've moved forty
times in my forty-nine years. That's some people's idea
of hell. But each time, the disruption makes me more
aware of who I am and what's around me. Changing
homes is mental as well as physical. Whether you're
moving up a floor, down the block, or to the other side
of the world, the transition is exhilarating. And exciting. And phenomenally stressful. ___Moving countries
is moving on steroids. When I moved to Australia,
I was overwhelmed, again. New house, new light, new
sounds, new neighbourhood, new energy. All the usual
stuff but there was also something very deep. I love
the smell of Australia. I love the feel. I love feeling
what it's like instead of thinking what it's like. I experi-
enced everything as if for the first time, even the
aroma of coffee. ___Moving is an opportunity to shed.
Like a snake shedding a skin. Humans accumulate like
crazy, like magpies hoarding shiny objects. The stress
for me in moving is not the finding of the new place,
but the reflection on the recent past, looking at my life
and the soon-to-be-ex-houseful of acquisitions, of
objects. You're forced to let it go – at least some of it.
___That's what I love about design. Any new brief is
a fresh injection, it's an opportunity to move mental
house. It's critical to repositioning, reorganizing and
re-casting an identity. Designing is about redesigning.
Creating a new way to see. Just because it's always
been this way doesn't mean it has to stay this way ●

DESIGNING IS ABOUT RE- DESIGNING CREATING A NEW WAY TO SEE

DESIGN YOUR SPACE

081

Type Bandit by Vince Frost 2009

ONLY THE LOVE WITHIN THE HOUSE CAN MAKE IT TRULY A HAPPY PLACE

Megan Morton, Stylist

Box #3, Mark Collis, 2007

over time, the things we collect can make our lives feel heavy

don't hoard crap

A Simple Beautiful Life

Natalie Slessor is Head of Workplace at Lend Lease. She has over 15 years experience in property strategy and managing the design process, and specific expertise on the workplace design of the future.

Natalie Slessor

INTERVIEW 02:

How important is it to create a positive environment at home, work or both?

It's incredibly important. A home is an expression of who you are. For me, it's a powerful tool to communicate to my kids, family and friends how I live, how I want to live and what I feel. It's always amazing to me how little I need to feel at home and comfortable, but the few things I do need are so fundamental. Humans are like pot plants – we need light and air and love. Property industries have spent a lot of time creating places that are commoditised and in some way inhuman because they deprive us of choice, which is so important. Often now, the design solutions for the workplaces of the future are not increasingly trendy, they're actually quite simple but what's being layered into them is an element of human choice. The workplaces that have designated areas for particular tasks or force people together or apart are the workplaces that are dying off. At home, people are also starting to challenge open-plan living; rooms are coming back to create a sense of division and choice. It all comes down to light, air, care and attention, and choice.

How do you design a work environment at home without it looking like an office?

This is a very interesting area. Flexible work patterns are increasing, particularly in a city like Sydney, which is incredibly expensive and both partners often need to work. The issue is that home is often not a great place to work. We've found that people working from home a lot start to feel isolated and cut off from colleagues, team members or the work itself. We're seeing a lot of corporates signing up for co-working centres in suburban areas of Sydney, so people can pop in and work together, are close to home but not at home. The way we work has changed so much, and technology has helped us a lot of course – in some ways you can call anywhere you like a workplace. Most Gen Y's will want to behave more like freelancers, not just in terms of mobility but also in terms of autonomy and wanting to be value driven. So it's interesting to see this whole new breed of space happening.

How are these spaces designed?

I think we're converging on something you might call "homely", a bit more humane, a lot more character and less systems-furniture and white laminate. There are elements of self-organising about them, often play-based, which allow for flexibility rather than a permanent design. I think the definition of design is that it does exactly what it should do and is beautiful and simple at the same time, so these things aren't mutually exclusive. If you accept the premise that design is meant to function supremely well, then a part of design is allowing for change. If it stays the same, it simply becomes an artefact.

Have you ever created a temporary home in an unexpected place?

I feel Australia's my temporary home after twelve years. My concept of home has really wandered and now it's more about who I'm with. I don't feel either English or Australian. Over the last few years in particular, I've found that my best creative thinking, ideas and experiences often happens in transit. Breaking the routine exposes you to new stimulus, it gives you energy and clarity and switches something on in your brain and if I couldn't do that, I wouldn't feel happy at all. It sounds a bit trite, but I think home is also a state of mind – having a sense of self-worth is a big part of it.

Do we need to unlearn certain traditions at home if we're to embrace this more fluid way of living?

Yes, and it starts with not just what the answers are but what the question is. For me for example, the question is not how do we eat together, it's how can we talk more as a family, how can I know more about my kids' lives, how can I share what's happening in my life and impart my wisdom and learning? By getting the question right, I've begun to understand that in my family, a mealtime is actually not the place to do any of this: my son hoovers up his food, my daughter takes forever, my husband and I work full time – it doesn't work, so we'll go for a walk instead. It doesn't have to break down traditional values, it's about trying to understand what you want to achieve and living by the principles of "How can I do this?"

Kids are naturally playful – hungry to learn and explore. Do you agree that school can sometimes kill aspects of their natural expression?

You're right. What's happening in curriculum-driven schools is that we really only teach two things: English and memory. We teach people to write about history, geography or science and remember as much as they can. We don't teach geography outside, we don't always teach science in laboratories. It's based on writing and remembering and funnelling kids to the HSC. The creative process is being lost. It's a real shame but I wouldn't know where to start. I just try and look for "effort points" – it doesn't matter if you're good or bad, effort and attitude is everything in this life. Find the thing you love and stick at it.

What do the words "design your life" mean to you?

I love the terminology. For me, it's about finding the questions, not the answers and living by the principles of discovery. Personally, I have a "vision question" for my life, not a "vision". It's "How can I have a positive impact on people's lives and the environment?" rather than, "I'm going to…" The principles of discovery for me are living by empathy, curiosity, being able to see simplicity through complexity, and understanding what real design and beauty is. So I think "design your life" is about positivity and control, it's about saying "What questions am I going to try to answer?" Questions like "Where do I want to live?" "Where do I want to travel?" "What's my purpose?" and living by the discoveries you make along the way. Above all else, try to find the thing you love – passion is always the best motivator.

With more and more emphasis on minimal living, is there any room for hoarding? Can it ever be a positive thing?

That's an interesting question. My husband is a bit of a hoarder, he used to be an engineer and loves to make stuff, so his tools are everywhere. I always want to get rid of it but he wants the kids to know how to make stuff. His breadth of stuff, which I think is hoarded, each part of it actually has a purpose and I started to think that something would be lost unless we keep some of the past somewhere. Now my son can do a bit of joinery and my daughter makes her own art canvases and it's better than them staring at the iPad. So perhaps some of the art of life is potentially being lost by not having that creative stuff around, and having kids certainly draws you down that road, suddenly you're surrounded by crates of it. Creative hoarding and preserving the past isn't a bad thing for work and play – I see a lot of work environments going towards creative thinking spaces that are very low tech, and give you a kit of parts that are physical rather than just a shiny screen on the wall and a teleconference phone. These spaces are more self-organising with things like Plasticine, white boards and all sorts of things. It's going back to the future slightly, but a lot of businesses are embracing the idea that touching stuff can help us to think a little more creatively ●

make sure you design your home for your personal wellbeing

Design needs to be sustainable. The body is a piece of design. You need to be sustainable. It's simple: the healthiest bodies function the best. The most functional design works the best. If you are fit and healthy, you are striking out unnecessary issues or complications. Functioning better makes your life easier. Still, it's not that simple. We put a lot of crap in our bodies. Being bad (alcohol, cigarettes, crap food, sleeping in) is easy. Being good (exercise, healthy eating, early mornings) is hard. People binge on wellbeing. They don't train or live for ongoing wellbeing. It's bloody hard. Find a balance between your everyday life, your family, your career and your health. Design yourself a more sustainable body. It will last longer.

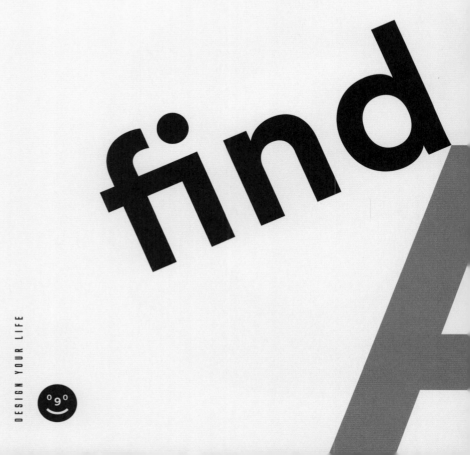

balance

I HAVE TO FIX MY WHOLE LIFE RIGHT NOW!

If you've ever had too much to drink you'll be familiar with the hangover. And you'll be familiar with the slow, surging euphoria of recovery as the pain passes and the body begins to crave input. ___Do what you love. Love what you do. Easy to say. Hard to do. How did we ever get to this state? The desire for more than we should have. One more glass of wine, one more serving of dessert, one more wafer-thin mint. ___The man-made world is toxic. Financial pressure. Road congestion. Air pollution. Mind pollution. We are bombarded by messages telling us what to desire and convincing us that we need it. There's an abundance but there's never enough. We self-sabotage. Most of us wait until we hit the wall before we think about changing. I did. I self-medicated with alcohol; one glass of wine becomes two becomes a bottle becomes two bottles. ___At first, I thought it was just another bout of man-flu. "Man-flu" was my semi-annual crisis. My body telling me to stop. A message from the shop floor telling me to lay down the tools. In bed drained of all vitality. When I did finally drag my sorry arse out of bed, I would look in the mirror and say, "Jesus." But then I'd feel better and just jump back into it. ___I would use it as a chance to take stock. At least I thought I was. Then one flu came and went but I didn't quite recover. I felt terrible, and there was a knock-on effect. I was emitting toxicity to the world. People were asking me: "Are you OK?" "You're a bit snappy." ___Frost* worked with Oz Harvest, an Australian charity that redistributes excess food. Seven billion tons of food is wasted every year in Australia. One in every five shopping bags is put in the bin. Supermarkets donate food that has reached its sell-buy date or is damaged and Oz Harvest distributes it to the hungry. Our design for the Oz Harvest brief focused on showing how many of us are unthinking consumers of food, of clothes, of cars, of everything. ___And there it was right in front of me. We were helping Oz Harvest with their message and I wasn't seeing it myself. I was overweight. My cholesterol was sky-high. I said to myself, "I have to fix my

City to Surf fun run 6 a.m. start at Hyde Park, Sydney

YOUR STOMACH IS THE SAME SIZE AS YOUR FIST

whole life right now." Which was ridiculous. But it was a start. I went to see a naturopath. Went to a doctor. I had a battery of tests done. We established the ideal body weight target. I went to a dietician. I started putting my fist up against my plate. Each meal you eat should be no more than the size of your stomach. The stomach is the same size as your fist. The idea of a diet sounded too much like a punishment, so I changed my approach to meals; nothing was banned, I just reduced the serving sizes. I didn't set up myself up for failure; that just leads to constant cravings. ___I started going to the gym. Bad news: You cannot be your designed body weight in two weeks. I imagined myself running marathons. I was tempted to go the whole hog, buy the shiny Olympian look, but I realized all I needed was a good pair of running shoes. I did the most natural thing we can do: I started walking, one determined foot after the other, around Centennial Park in Sydney. It felt good. ___Finding that balance is a life-long challenge. It's not easy. But it's simple. I established the best possible outcome and worked towards it. It took me a year to get fit – well, fit-ish ●

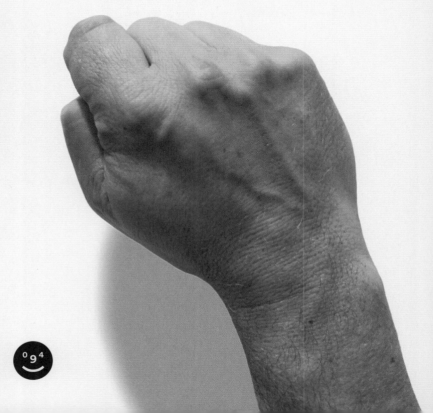

ONE BOTTLE OF WINE =

SLICES OF BREAD!

Cumeless

we don't need as much as we think we do in our lives

Changing Habits

Gabriela Rosa is a clinician, author and internationally recognised naturopath and fertility specialist. She holds a Master of Science in Medicine (Reproductive Health and Human Genetics) from Sydney University and a Bachelor of Health Science. She practises from her Natural Healing Centre in Sydney.

Gabriela Rosa

INTERVIEW 03:

How important is it to "be present"?
It's vital. People come into my clinic with anxiety, depression or feeling like the world is against them and what it really comes down to is two things: the first is that nothing is as bad as we make it out to be in our minds. Secondly, not being present allows our minds to create things that aren't there and alter our reality. Being present keeps you focused and immediately stops your mind creating horror stories. For example, doing something as simple as feeling the sensation of your feet brings you back into your body and helps you become more present in the moment. Being present in your mind and body can make a huge difference to anxiety and be absolutely life changing in so many other ways.

Do you believe in collaboration, rather than going it alone?
I absolutely believe that and it's something I've learnt through my own experience. When I first started my business, I was a sole practitioner doing what I knew to help people and grow my business. I very quickly realised that I didn't actually have all of the skills I needed and wanted to make my business the success that I envisioned in my mind. I required more knowledge and expertise and if I was to become the person I needed to be in order to achieve my goals, I had to ask for the help and support of people who had already done what I wanted to do.

Once I knew that I was accountable to someone else, I also found I pushed myself harder. I now see this with my patients – if they have a goal then I see them weekly because if they know they need to report regularly, they're more likely to stick at it. Asking for help is often the easy part, it's understanding that you need it that's difficult.

Being healthy can be hard – things that are good for you seem harder to do, and bad things seem more attractive. What do you make of this?
Here's the thing: human beings become slaves to habits and unless we make those habits good ones, there's going to be demise in some shape or form. I truly believe that's why we struggle – our habits are not life supporting or health promoting, so we bypass logic in that day-to-day action. As children we have impulses; then we start to learn that actions cause reactions, and we start to mould our actions based on our beliefs and attitudes. Some people, through education, parenting or other means, start to develop habits that aren't beneficial because they've never been encouraged otherwise. In the long term, it depends on that person to make changes – as soon as we can differentiate between right and wrong, that's when we have the ability to choose what we're going to focus on. Changing habits can take a few attempts or it can take a lifetime – you just have to be truly committed to making it happen.

Do you believe it's possible to "design your life"?
There's a quote along the lines of "When the student is ready, the teacher appears", and the teacher can come in many forms – a book, person, an event. It comes down to being ready. If we make the commitment to design our lives and actually live the life that we truly envision in our minds that we will live, the only thing that separates the person who will do it from the person who will still be talking about it in ten years' time is Eric Thomas' quote, "When you want to succeed as badly as you want to breathe, then you will be successful". It's the only thing that differentiates the two. Anything in life that you want – to design a better life, to be healthier, to have better relationships – you have to really want it. That's what I'm helping people to do, find that inner strength and desire to transition from where they are to where they want to be.

How many people think it's possible to actively "design your life" versus thinking that life just happens?
We can control only one thing in our lives – how we choose to think about things. Everything else is completely out of our control. We all go through pleasant or unpleasant situations in life, but it all depends on how you choose to think about it. The second we focus our attention on how things aren't how we want them to be, guess what? That's the time we become victims to our reality, as opposed to making our own reality. I truly believe with every fibre in my being that I am the decider of my destiny, irrespective of what happens in my life, it's up to me to navigate towards the outcome that I want. I think Zig Ziglar said it best, "It's not what we get in life by achieving our goals, it's who we become by achieving our goals" ●

TO DESIGN A BETTER LIFE, TO BE HEALTHIER, TO HAVE BETTER RELATIONSHIPS YOU HAVE TO REALLY WANT IT

pace yo u r

s e l f

slow and steady wins the race

instead of meeting in an office talk and walk

walk

talk

walk

walk

walk

walk

talk

walk

walk

walk

walk

talk

talk

To solve the problem you need to fully understand it, and to understand it you have to ask a lot of questions. When a brief comes into the studio, the first thing we do is ask a stream of questions: "What, why, how?" We gather information to find out as much as we can to create an intelligent solution. If you ask yourself, "Why am I doing this?", "How do I want to live?", the answer isn't as important as the question. Because the question itself means you recognise a moment of potential change. Simply, there is an alternative. You don't have to be like this. You can find a happier, more successful state.

This is design at its best. Design allows this dog to get around and enjoy life on the South Bank, London

The humble question mark: A stroke and a dot creates a universe. A lightning strike. Over the centuries the symbol has taken on a life of its own. The Japanese and Chinese have now embraced it in their character set. In Arabic, which reads right to left, the question mark is the mirror image. It's a universal symbol. ? ___ Fill in the blank. ___Who. What. Where. When. Easy to ask. Easy to answer. ___Why. A little word that asks so much. Three letters. So many possibilities. ___As a designer I question things constantly. 'Why' asks us to delve deep, to tap for answers. 'Why' is about getting information. We set out on a quest for an answer. The brief lays out the quest, and we begin to ask questions: what are the different ways to express the potential solutions? It's simple. We do what any good designer does. We take an opportunity and turn it into something that is unique to the situation.

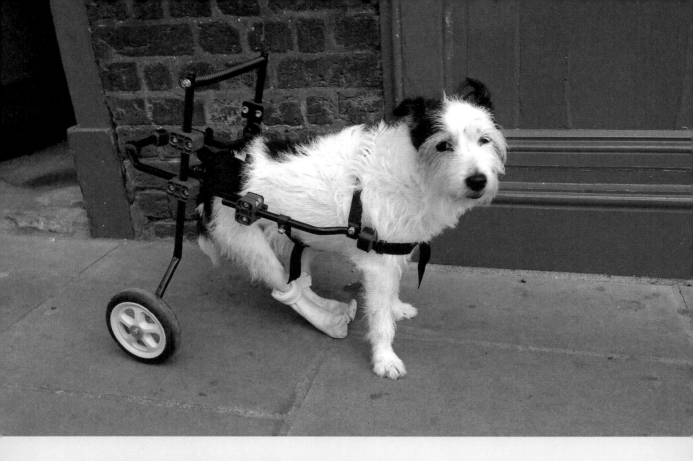

___Why is a gateway to possibility. Why is the door to a solution. Turn it around. Q: What happens if you don't ask why? A: Nothing. ___It's human nature to question any situation. ___To question means to see everything around you. It means being open to and engaged with your environment. That's how we find scenarios for making things better ⬢

JUDGMENT IS CONCERNED WITH "WHAT IS" DESIGN IS CONCERNED WITH "WHAT COULD BE"

Edward deBono

the more you know the better informed you are

g
e

Q

How many designers does it take to change a light bulb?

A

Does it have to be a light bulb?

Prediction

Chris Sanderson is co-founder and CEO of The Future Laboratory and the online trends and insight network, LSNGlobal.com.

Chris Sanderson

INTERVIEW 04:

What does "design your life" mean to you?
Really, design is about thinking about something from the inside out, from the bottom up; the whole process from start to finish, integrating your experience and making it coherent. It means that you take something to pieces with the intention of working out how to put it back together again; the result is that it functions better and is a better-looking object as well. Designing your life is taking the time to think very carefully about what the job is, what you want it to achieve, what you want to get out of it, and planning according to those concerns, rather than just seeing things happen. It's about the measure of control that you take.

Do you feel as if you've designed your life?
I feel I've been in control. Ageing is a pretty amazing thing, but it also plays quite a few tricks on you. There were a couple of very conscious decisions I made when I was younger about what I wanted to do, what I wanted to be, and what I didn't want to be. And those have had an enormous impact on who I am today.

One of the things I learnt very early was that you should never blame anyone else for anything you did or did not do. I'm the one controlling my destiny and my fate and it's pretty much up to me as to why things did or did not happen.

And as you age, you might look at decisions you made twenty years ago and think, well, maybe that wasn't such a great decision; I could have done things differently, but at least you were the one who made those decisions and acted on them, however wise or unwise.

Do you think that there is a country where people are living a better-designed life? In your trend analysis, do you see any particular country that has got it more right than others?
Yes – if you look at Scandinavia, it enjoyed a post-war boom and it was able to take good design skills and apply them to manufacturing at an affordable level which could be embraced by the majority of the population. There's also social planning, which is when you see design really, really work there. You see that sensibility coming through and the novelty is still there and it still resonates.

And it could still be taken more seriously by most governments and politicians, when it comes to thinking about how to make a city a better place to live and work in. Because whilst social experimentation can also go wrong, and we're all aware of urban planning that has been a total disaster, where the life and soul have been ripped out of a community through unnecessary or bad social planning, there are also obviously instances where it works, when you see something that is created that has a lasting impact on the community and/or society as it grows and changes.

Analysts at The Future Laboratory create visual cartograms that help map the future for a client

THE "WHY" IS TO ME THE MOST IMPORTANT QUESTION RATHER THAN THE "WHAT"

And what about one's own wellbeing, so it goes deeper, about finding out who you are, focusing on what is your centre, your purpose? Potentially reprogramming yourself, redesigning yourself to create better outcomes in your life.

To me, at the heart of design is thought; being thoughtful, because without thoughtfulness, design doesn't work. Design is an art; it is not simply about intuition or expression; design is about careful, thoughtful planning.

It's all about the process, a series of thoughtful actions. You can take that element of design and be more mindful, you can be more careful, you can kind of do whatever you want, to some extent. But you've actually made a decision ahead of that, in terms of what you want to do or what you want to achieve, what the outcome might be. That process can apply to whatever area of your life you want it.

How's the best way for someone who's stuck to get into that frame of mind? What would unblock them, what would make them embrace what you just said?
I think one of the things is understanding how you think about wiping the slate clean, how you think about removing bad design and the bits that aren't working. And one of the most interesting things about the human condition is that a lot of parts of our bodies are actually designed to self-replicate, to reproduce, and may not necessarily carry any residual memory of things that have happened before. We have a remarkable capacity to heal. And learning how to allow yourself to renew, to refresh, is the most important part, and also the most difficult because it involves letting go. It's about how I let go of the past hurt or the past damage and allow my body to renew or to refresh. And that's the bit that most of us find really difficult because there are parts of ourselves that don't want to do that, because often the pain is also part of what makes me what I am.

Did you find your career actively or did you stumble across it? Because it's obviously something that makes you; you seem to be motivated by what you do. Do you get a lot of pleasure out of it and enjoy it full-heartedly, or is it just a job for you?
Early on I had a couple of moments where I realised that there was a career path that I was set on but it just wasn't going to work for me. And I had to think about what I really wanted to do. And I still don't have all the answers for that. I certainly don't know if I'm going to be doing what I'm currently doing for the rest of my life. I have no idea what I might be doing in ten years' time. But I'm really happy that I don't know that, and one of the exciting things is finding out: so, what do I want to do on the next journey, in the next part of my life?

But I did learn, very early on, a couple of what my core competencies were, and I was able to build a business around those. One was that I am an ideas person and I was lucky enough to have somebody who told me very early on that that was a great quality to have.

The second was being curious; I'm incredibly inquisitive about people and what makes them tick. And the third was understanding that I'm a good communicator, and appreciating those qualities meant I could look around and think, what can I do that can build on those three core skills? And that's what I've done.

You have literally designed your life based on your core skills.
There wasn't an industry, then, based around forecasting or prediction. There was within the tiny niche of fashion, and there were businesses that supported the fashion industry, but that was kind of it. And for us it was a lightbulb moment of understanding that what we'd learnt working in the fashion industry was something we could take to other industries.

It sounds perfectly tailored to your core skills.
As you grow the business, you realise your core skills might be fantastic but you also learn what your core weaknesses are, the bits that are missing, and that doesn't come straight away. And that's almost

as important as recognising your core skills because you've then got to find the people who complement you. That takes a little bit more work and normally a few fuck-ups along the way.

I'm interested when you mention you're a curious person. Do you think that just a human trait; are we all like that or are there certain types of people who question everything and look for answers, trying to improve the world individually?
I think there are plenty of people who aren't particularly curious. Often as you age you just accept more; that's the way it is, that's the way things work, instead of constantly going, why does it have to be that way? The "why" is to me the most important question rather than the "what", because it questions how things work, the underpinning mechanism, the organisational system, or the structure.

That's what we try to make different with the way we work for our clients; we saw all sorts of organisations, and there are many around still, that are very good at identifying things for you and showing them to you. But for us, we wanted to create a business that was answering the "why" question and delivering insight to you, helping you to understand why this is important and then follow on with questions of what that might mean to you. And so for us, it's about insight and ensuring you're not just able to demarcate the difference between one thing and another, you're actually able to show and explain why this thing is important and help people to understand the impact of that difference or that newness.

We're talking about companies on the whole, but how could an individual get this information? Where would one go?
I think answers mostly lie in a decent bookshop. I'm old-fashioned! It's all there and often what we need to do is locate the books that suit us because no one's got the time or the energy to read from every philosophy, but everyone can find a few people who make sense to them.

And for me, that's a really important thing, just finding the particular voices that actually strike a chord for you. And then the rest of it is actually applying yourself to spend the time to allow these things to permeate, to allow yourself the time to think and study, to engage, to read, to meditate on something. I don't mean that in a formal, structured way, just allow your brain the time to engage with another idea or concept you hadn't considered.

I think often it's really simple things like that, that we often think are a bit crazy, a bit silly or just a bit wanky really, but really make such a massive difference to your day.

If you don't take those minutes, step away from the desk, if you don't actually take time to have lunch properly, to just engage in a conversation with a colleague about something that's completely different, then you're not challenging yourself. You need to pay attention to other stuff that's going on around you, whether that be politics, gossip, sports — all of those things help to supply context and meaning.

Especially now with this endless 24/7 bombardment of content which actually just eats away at you. You think you need to be part of it somehow, or you're going to miss out if you don't connect or Tweet or whatever, but it's incredibly exhausting. I think that people are waking up to that fact that they're just not shutting off and that really starts to play on your wellbeing, big time.

That is one of the obsessions of our age. And again, it's particular to our generation I think, because all of the technological changes and advancements that have happened in our lifetime are new for us and so we obsess about them. Whereas one of the great things about watching a child now with technology is how they treat it, like a light switch, to be turned on and off as they need. It's seamless for them. And that's fantastic. It's our generation that obsesses about the technology and how to use it, whereas for the young generation it's just there ●

positive

negative

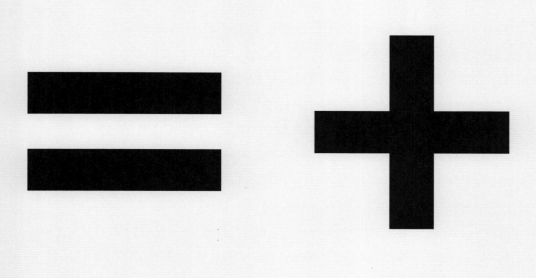

you get back what you give out

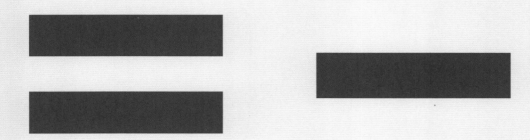

It's hard to collaborate with yourself. In fact, you can't, unless you have multiple personalities. No one person knows everything and the world can be a lonely place if you're thinking about stuff by yourself. Collaborating with others takes the pressure off and helps you see things you might otherwise be blind to. Bouncing ideas off diverse people – pooling resources, wisdom, flavours, opinions and experiences – creates debate, insight, and friction – all good grounds for finding the best possible outcome. Equally, though, don't collaborate just for the sake of it. Work out which projects are actually going to benefit from collaboration before inviting others to get involved.

THERE'S ZERO CORRELATION BETWEEN BEING THE BEST TALKER AND HAVING THE BEST IDEAS

Susan Cain, Author of *Quiet*

By nature I'm an introvert. It comes from a lifetime of listening to and observing what's around me. I wasn't trained to run a business. Or to delegate. People always said collaboration was a good thing. I wasn't sure what collaboration meant: perhaps commissioning an illustrator, or a photographer. For me, design was about doing it myself. ___A lot of designers I know are introverted. They are the last people to want to collaborate. They enjoy the alone time, the pleasure and satisfaction of being fully absorbed in a task. Sharing to them would be a dilution or a compromise. But there has been a big shift away from the guru solo designer going away and having that eureka moment. The current buzzword is "design thinking": the notion that you can fill a room with creative people and get them bouncing around like molecules in a pot until the room boils over with… Ideas? Not necessarily. ___Collaboration may be too grand a term for what happens in some workshops. My sceptical antennae buzz whenever I hear the phrase "blue sky thinking". A brainstorming session can produce crappy weather. You can have a boardroom table crowded with people who don't have a lot of insight. Those who aren't comfortable being quiet fill the air and change the direction, affect the outcome. People think someone who is loud and confident is good, because they take the lead in a convincing way. ___"There's zero correlation between being the best talker and having the best ideas." Susan Cain, Author ___And the quiet ones sit there wishing they were somewhere else, away from this collective one-track mind. Creators often go through their own process of finding an original idea before opening their mouths, and may stumble in pressured situations. I see them as I scan the faces, the people who hesitate to voice their opinion. And that doesn't go down well in business. Yet it's often where the discoveries are made. Just sitting alone, thinking "What if?", sketching, can tap into things that would never have come from conversation. Lateral thinking leads to happy accidents.

There's a tension between the power of groups and the power of solitary thinking. Between the introverts and extroverts, and everybody in between. True collaboration is a shared commitment to tap into ideas. To listen purposefully. To speak purposefully. Work with peers who feel comfortable challenging you. Equally, though, if you know your idea is good, don't be discouraged by others if you don't think their criticism is valid. And even if you're not mad about an idea, don't shoot it down. Too many ideas are killed before they get a chance to breathe. Learn from others and tease out clues to solving the problem. ___I used to want to be the one who owned the best idea, now I don't care as long as it's great. For example, Frost* was commissioned to design the look and feel of a cancer centre. The stakes were enormous. The centre would be filled with people in crisis. People in fear. All the stakeholders were around the table: the client, the marketing team, the potential audience, designers, strategists, people from the university, the hospital administration, doctors, nurses, sponsors. Everyone had different opinions, some of them contradictory. Our strategists and designers were ready to challenge them, and they did. No one was spared. But by having that openness and transparency – where everyone has an opportunity to say and share – it's almost like mediation. It strengthens the group. We helped them articulate their vision. We helped them help us. ___It's a very different process to doing it by yourself. Other people fill the gaps – and more. You need to bring other people into your life to make it full. To fulfill your potential ●

TRUE
COLLABORATION
IS
A
SHARED
COMMITMENT
TO
TAP
INTO
IDEAS

te

am

i

there is no i in team

Creative Business

Roy Green is the Dean of the UTS Business School at the University of Technology, Sydney.

Professor Roy Green

INTERVIEW 05:

What does "Design Your Life" mean to you?
I think it's another way of asking what is your life plan, and some people have them, but most don't. Most have aspirations and I think that's something that we should all have, but how we deliver them is not something that can easily be designed, although you can build structure and sequence into realising your ambition.

I can't say that this is something that I've done personally to any great extent. Much of what I do is opportunistic. It is operating within an overall framework, but takes advantage of opportunities as I find them rather than trying to structure them in advance. We do have to take advantage of what we see around us and act accordingly.

Marx said something like: people make their own history, but they don't make it in circumstances of their own choosing. In other words, there is a relationship between human agency and the structures in which we operate. This has long been a subject of philosophy and sociology, and it's about the role of individuals in history and the effect of the material economic conditions that provide opportunities, or deny them to us.

Designing one's life in this context is an enormously challenging concept because it assumes that those circumstances are not necessarily given, but can be manipulated, but that is less and less likely to be the case for most people. It is a question of how we make the best of the cards which we are dealt.

I guess what we're trying to get across is for people to have a feeling that life doesn't just happen to them, and they actually can take control of their wellbeing and environment.
I think individuals can certainly gain much greater control over their own lives and life chances, and it is clearly advisable to do so. No one wants to be a victim of circumstances. We want to influence in ways that add to our personal advantage and to the advantage of people from our community, but there are limits and these are often imposed by the workplace, in which little democracy or empowerment exists.

Certainly, in enlightened workplaces, employers realise that drawing on talent and releasing creativity is the key to innovation and progress, but in so many other workplaces today, people are operating within mini-dictatorships. I think this is something which ought to be addressed by society because we're not drawing sufficiently on people's talents unless they are empowered to make a difference.

You seem to be doing a lot with students and teachers, and in business. How do you find the right people to collaborate with?
Collaboration is the essence of making any kind of progress. We cannot make progress without productive interaction with our colleagues, our students and sometimes with external partners.

Collaboration is essential both to the development of ideas and their execution. People generally accept that you cannot implement an idea successfully unless you have some form of structured collaboration, but fewer people are fully aware of the role of collaboration in developing ideas in the first place. This is increasingly the case in industry and in all walks of life; that ideas and innovation are driven more and more by collaborative thought processes and activities. The idea of the solo individual inventor or innovator is becoming a thing of the past.

We have a frontier mentality still. We have this folk memory about inventing the stump-jump plough and the Hill's Hoist, and even more recently, Australian inventions such as the black box flight recorder, Relenza, wi-fi. These all originated from this country. Some of them were commercialised offshore, some of them were developed and commercialised here, but most of them are seen as solo runs. They're isolated examples of success. They're not part of what other countries view as emerging innovation ecosystems.

That is where collaboration really has an impact. Once you develop a network of interconnections, this is what becomes an innovation ecosystem. Then you make progress not just with your ideas, but also with the execution of those ideas, the transformation of those ideas into commercial products or in the community, the translation of ideas into social benefit – because not all ideas need to be driven by profit. Some of them can and should operate in the public sphere and advance the interests of whole communities.

How do you decide when you need to collaborate and when it's better to do it yourself?
Individuals will always generate ideas and a vision of the future. The point is that there are plenty of people who can develop a fine vision, but without a genuine sense of collaboration, and without the empathy which shapes collaboration, many of these ideas may fall on rocky ground. Many of them do.

COLLABORATION IS THE ESSENCE OF MAKING ANY KIND OF PROGRESS

Model of Dr Chau Chak Wing Building by Gehry Partners LLP

Some people think collaboration is compromise. Do you think that if you get ten people in a room and not one person owns the idea, do you think you'd still get a strong outcome?
That's a good question and there's quite a controversy in the literature; there's a backlash now against brainstorming. There was an interesting article recently – I think it was in *The New Yorker* – pointing to all the negative connotations of brainstorming, or "groupthink" as it was described, that a bunch of people, without any clear idea of what they want to achieve, think that if they sit in a room for long enough and write inanities on Post-it notes, a brilliant concept will somehow emerge for their product, for their business or for their community.

You do not necessarily guarantee an outcome through collaboration, and I can see that side of the argument. But true, well-structured collaboration, which isn't a set of compromises but is building layers of ideas, does produce beneficial and sometimes inspiring results, whether in relation to a technological breakthrough, a new business model, a new way of organising within the business, a new way of accessing a global value chain.

Sometimes these approaches are labelled design-led innovation because they require a degree of design thinking, asking managers and professionals to think like designers. We don't always do that in strategic management. If we think like a designer with a blank page we might ask, "Where does this business want to be in five years? How do we want customers to visualise our products and services? How do we know that we're going to be successful?" It's a method of thinking rather than a formula, in a collaborative context, and some genuinely productive ideas can emerge with the potential to create value.

So with the new business school that you're building, you've introduced design thinking into the curriculum, and you're building an amazing Frank Gehry building. How did that collaboration between business and design come about?
Five years ago now, we asked ourselves, "Where would we want to be as a business school in five or ten years?" We have around 300 academic and professional staff, and we wanted it to be a democratic process in which everyone had a voice.

We wanted to hear The Voice of Experience, The Voice of the Future, and so on, and people worked in constantly changing groups to provide a balanced representation of all of these different elements. These views ultimately coalesced into the direction we would like to go.

During this "strategic conversation" as we called it, we were about to put the new building out to public tender, but the prospect emerged of bringing in an architect who was very much aligned to the way of thinking we were evolving. And that was Frank Gehry. We shared our vision with him and were delighted to find that it resonated with his own philosophy of the future of education in general, and business education in particular. It started a productive and inspiring relationship between our university and this creative genius, who "designs from the inside out", as he puts it. He doesn't design a building to make it look aesthetically distinctive, although that is certainly one aspect of what he does. He designs with a view to the functionality of the spaces for the people who use it.

Is Frank a dictator or a collaborator?
You should ask his staff! Seriously, though, when you have such an authentic creative leader in charge of an organisation, of course his ideas must unfold to some degree from the relationships around him, which include his staff, but particularly his client. "Dictator" is the wrong word. The real dictators in architecture are those who think they know best and impose their will on the client, and on the community, and we've seen many such buildings with no understanding or sympathy with the surroundings, or indeed with the people who live and work in them.

This is the history of some of our appalling post-war architecture – buildings that gave such a bad name to modernism when the ethos and the principles of modernism were so different to start with. I think Gehry is following through the true principles of modernism, which are about form following function through collaboration, particularly with those who live and work in the buildings. That's why each of his buildings is different because he doesn't have a standard design formula except that he starts from the aspirations of the client, which may be a whole community, or as it is in our case, a community of academics and students.

We had a central organising idea about how the kind of interactive environment we wanted, in which people could engage with each other, might look, and he has made that reality. For this reason, Gehry has designed what he calls a "porous" building. Yes, he consults, he is a collaborator, but once he has an idea about something as a result of the collaboration, he follows it through and innovates relentlessly.

Do you believe in left-brain and right-brain thinkers?

I think we can see that in daily life such differences exist, but connections have to be found. You cannot force scientists to collaborate with people in the arts and humanities, or vice versa, but when they have the opportunity to do so, they produce some of the most interesting interdisciplinary work. We certainly want that to happen here in this building and in this university. That's one of the great strengths of UTS; people see the value of the whole being greater than the sum of the parts. That's what a really creative university can do and what it must do if it wishes to be relevant to modern businesses and communities, and to succeed in a competitive marketplace. Design thinking is that right-brain element of intuitive thinking, of empathy, and, on the other side, business analytics is about the more analytical frame of mind. This is the activity that grounds intuitive thinking in the realities of the marketplace, the realities of choice, the realities of strategy and of structure. It is the combination of these two ways of thinking that makes a successful company or organisation. Intuitive thinking on its own will have its limits, but so will analytical thinking.

A lot of people can go through their lives not fully understanding what their strengths are, and end up struggling through a career that's not right for them.

Yes, a lot of people are not recognised for the strengths that they have, and they often do not recognise it themselves. They cultivate strengths that they think people would like them to have, which may not really be the best use of their talents and potential. We're trying to train people in our business school with a combination of specialised knowledge, which we know is essential, with the boundary-crossing skills of communication, problem solving, and critical thinking. We want to create

what some call "T-shaped" graduates, who have not only the necessary deep knowledge of business domains but also the cross-cutting skills that employers are increasingly looking for, and also students who wish to create their own ventures.

And you don't have to go to a university to act on this? You can start doing it in your everyday life?

Absolutely. It is that ability to discover your own strengths that allows you to find someone who complements them. That is the essence of a truly successful collaboration, to recognise that if you are an intuitive thinker and you have gaps in analytics, that you can work with someone who complements your skills and vice versa because not everyone is going to encompass all of those different elements, however much they try. We are always going to have a bias to one set of skills over another. It is through self-reflection that we discover the value we bring to an organisation.

We are always going to have an emphasis on one set of skills over another. It is through the process of self-reflection that one discovers the advantage one brings to an organisation, whether it's one we work for or one that we create ourselves.

Do you think if people could design their lives, they would be happier?

I think all the research shows that workplaces and organisations where people have no control over their work lives tend to have higher rates of sickness, of mortality, of low morale, of absenteeism. We now try to design organisations that give people greater control, or at least enlightened organisations do so. Enlightened employers do so and everyone benefits as a result. Some degree of control or sense of direction is clearly required, but I don't personally believe people would be made happier by designing their lives as a purpose-built nirvana, because it leaves out some of the most wonderful aspects of life, which are produced by serendipity ●

bounceot

discover a new energy and stronger ideas

hers

ff

Ask why, don't ask why me? In life there are real victims. I have nothing but compassion for them. But there is one kind of person who makes me crazy. The Excuser. "It was the ref's fault." "I'm a Gemini." "I'm on the cusp." The Excuser doesn't take responsibility for the here and now. The Excuser relies on external forces to escape responsibility. But it's not an escape. It's a missed opportunity. Take responsibility. Learn from it. Say, "This is on me."

me)

I WOULD PRAY FOR A FIRE, OR A HURRICANE OR A TORNADO TO DESTROY MY SCHOOL

We dislike most what we dislike in ourselves. I was an excuser. I remember when I was kid, I was very scared before exams and I would pray for a fire, or a hurricane or a tornado to destroy my school. Of course it never happened. ___I've seen excusers in the workplace. A designer I knew had been on a project for months and, oh, was he bitter. "The client is a prick." "The brief is idiotic." "The budget's too small." He blamed everyone and everything but bore none of the responsibility. The poor bastard. ___ I've been in client meetings with several designers around a table. And they didn't ask a single question. There was no determination to dig deeper. They'd set themselves up to fail. Meanwhile, the client ultimately pays the price.___I spent some time at a client's head office. Their design team had been given an assign-ment by one of the divisions. Ten months had passed and they were still struggling to find a solution. The head of the division was frustrated and threatening to hire an outside agency. The in-house design team was panicking. Their pride was at stake. Young and inex-perienced, they had been challenged with a straight-forward task and now they were going into a tailspin. ___I could see the solution. But I wasn't going to give it to them. I wanted to help them to find it themselves. We got everyone to step away from the situation and do a quick, ten-minute workshop. They got messy, with sketches and post-it notes. It freed everyone up and cleared the blocks, and sure enough, they found the solution. ___You set yourself up for excuses by not knowing what you want to achieve. A lack of vision. The clearer the goal, the more you accept it as a real-ity. If you're not committed, if you don't have faith that you can achieve it, then the finish line is never in sight. How could it be? You don't know where it is.

Canada after a storm. 1998

Own the opportunity. Say to yourself, "I'm going to be responsible for this and have the determination to make it great. If I have questions I'm going to ask questions because that will help me be great." This way, you get to challenge yourself. You get to contribute. You get to move things through. That's forward energy. ___Making excuses instead of getting down to work creates negative energy. It's the cliff edge. It's fear. It holds you back in life and stops you from being great. ___I can guarantee this: you'll feel better if you try than if you don't ●

IT'S NOT MY

~~JOB~~

I HAVE BIG

~~BONES~~

I LOST MY

~~WATCH~~

I'M

~~CU~~

THE CLIENT'S A

~~JERK~~

IT WASN'T

ME

IT WAS THE REF'S

FAULT

I'M A

GEMINI

THE

SP

THERE'S NOT ENOUGH

BUDGET TIME

love
over
hate

give

over

take

get the equation right

"Rather than life is something w accept, or endure.

something w

ccepting that
passively receive,
believe that life is
GENERATE."

Bruce Mau, Designer

trust the one person you can control

u

believe

<u>**Say "YES" and Mean It**</u>

"Yes" is a symbol of outward positivity. It's a willingness to connect with something that comes your way – in business or in your personal life. It means you are present and open to change and unforeseen opportunities. However, meaning it is equally important. Don't promise things you can't deliver. Set yourself achievable goals to help you deliver success.

DESIGN YOUR LIFE

PEACE + LOVE

THE MORE YOU ACCEPT THE GOAL AS A REALITY THE MORE LIKELY YOU ARE TO ACHIEVE IT

5

"ay yes to everything, and mean it. Easy for me to say. Every day in my studio, I say "yes". I shout it from the rooftops. "We can do it." But you have to be careful about what you're saying "yes" to. There is a tension between yes and no. ___In my business, the client makes the first move. They pick up the phone. They are looking for a collaborator. And they are asking you. That's the first buzz: you feel good that someone needs you. That someone is reaching out to you. Next: the opportunity intrigues you. So you commit. You say to the client: "I will do whatever it takes to make this a success but first you must define what makes a success to you." You need both parties' commitment to achieve a positive outcome. To define success you must both know what you want to achieve. Be on the same page. The clearer the goal, the more you accept it as reality, the more likely you are to achieve it.

TOUCH THE PUCK

SAY YES AND MEAN IT

___Families don't work this way. Especially children. They don't want you as a supplier. They don't want you as a marketer. They don't want to collaborate. It's not yesses all round. "You don't know what you're talking about, Dad." My kids tell me: "You're not the boss of me."

___Kid: "Stop telling me what to do."
___Me: "So what are you going to do?"
___Kid: "I don't know. But don't tell me what to do."

___I'm responsible for my kids' safety; I can see the dangers and pitfalls of things they might want to do that they can't. But at the same time, it is my job to support and encourage them, to help them grow and learn to be creative. To teach them to say "yes" to themselves. ___Chella Tingley, a coach of kids' hockey in Canada, has a very wise approach. Not every kid is a Wayne Gretsky. Not every kid is going to score a goal. Many little kids just drift around. But they're on the ice and that's a start. That's a "yes". So here's how she challenges them: "Touch the puck five times." They come off the ice: "I did it!" And then next game challenge them to touch the puck ten times.
___By setting achievable goals you help them say

'YES'.

saying yes creates a positive flow of energy

Giving From the Heart

Ronni Kahn is a social entrepreneur and
the founder of the food rescue charity,
OzHarvest.

Ronni Kahn

INTERVIEW 06:

**You seem to me to be a very positive person.
What's your outlook on life?**
Yes. Completely. I am a positive person. I think
attitude's about the most important thing we have,
and I realised it growing up. My dad was involved
in a very serious car accident when I was little.
And basically they didn't think he'd live through
the night, not to mention the week, and he landed
up in hospital for two years and it significantly
changed his life. But I only realised, when I did his
eulogy when he died, fifty years later, that actually
he was disabled; he just never thought of himself
as disabled, never behaved like someone who was
challenged, and so that's a pretty powerful role
model. My mum, whose life changed when her
husband suddenly was not able to earn, did all kinds
of jobs, from baking a hundred cakes a day to selling
encyclopaedias and wallpaper, anything that she
could – and I never once saw them not smiling.

So I was brought up around positivity and making
the best of it, and knowing there's always somebody
worse off and we've got so much to be grateful
about, and that's really my philosophy.

**And were you aware of that as a kid or you just
took it as that's how it was?**
As a kid I just took that as the norm, but as I grew
older and wiser I started realising what a gift I'd
been given. And the interesting thing is I'd always
thought it was my mum because she just was really
this smiley, happy, bright person. My dad was much
quieter, but he was actually the most positive person
because he never let his physical disabilities stop
him. He could have just sat at home but he climbed
up ladders and had his car adapted and he operated
as a fully functioning human being. So that affected
me on a subliminal level. Once I became aware of it,
I realised that it's actually the most precious thing
that we have.

When did you realise that?
Well, my mum had worked all her life for when they
would retire and then she got cancer and died very
young, at 63. And I realised that through her illness,
she still had that strength. As I matured I realised that
strength of character and positivity are hugely important. I've made changes in my life; I've emigrated
twice; I ended up here with a family, with no money,
but it was perfect, it was just what I needed to do.

How important is it to have a positive attitude?
I think it's actually the most fundamental thing; to
me it's as core as having food on your table because
if you don't, god, I can't imagine how miserable life
would be. If you can't find joy, how do you manage
when things go wrong? So things to me are challenges, not obstacles; it's about finding the best way
to get through things.

OzHarvest annual report designed by Frost*

DELIVERING
GOODNESS

Annual Report 2012

Are you positive all the time, or only when you're on show?

I'm pretty much like this all the time, so you can imagine how difficult that is for people to live with! It is good, but sometimes people want to switch off the Energiser Bunny.

"Stop being so positive all the time!"

Yeah. But I cannot wake up and not say what a magnificent day and how lucky I am to be here. I live life very much in the present. That started with my mum's death. She'd spent her life thinking about retiring, and then she died. So I'm going to make the best and most of what I have right now. I'm very conscious of living now.

That's wonderful advice. If someone was finding it difficult to be positive can you give them any advice that would help them change that?

I think we have a choice. I think absolutely the biggest gift is when we realise we have a choice: to wake up and be grumpy or to wake up and be happy. When you realise that actually it is completely up to us, it's very empowering.

And what's the process you go through before you say yes to something? When do you say no?

Boundaries are really important. I have started saying no so that I can preserve the power of yes. But it doesn't take a long process; I am very visceral and if something's put to me and it makes sense, I find a way of making it happen.

You started OzHarvest because you saw a cause and thought, I can make this happen; what if I could help someone?

It never occurred to me that I couldn't, actually. I never spent one minute thinking "What if I fail?" I just knew that I could do something that would be impactful in this space.

What gave you that insight or that confidence?

That confidence comes from having knowledge of one's skills, capacity, strengths and weaknesses. I knew that I'd need to garner help and support, and once you recognise that you can take the strengths you've got and then surround yourself with the strength that you lack; that's also very empowering. And people are drawn to conviction and passion. I'm constantly amazed by that magnetic force that OzHarvest has.

So what made you start it?

I wanted to know what it would feel like to make a difference to millions of people. Other than just living for myself. I did have a life change in that I was in a relationship with someone who was seemingly very rich; I'll never know if he was or wasn't but we certainly lived as if he was, and I'd never had money. And I discovered that having money didn't come with values, and I realised that I needed to put into practice what was important to me. I realised that actually I was about more than just needing money.

Did you kind of hit a wall to have that realisation?

Well, my life seemed to have everything that I'd always thought was important, and then I realised that actually, you know, I thought everything would be different when I had money, and then when I had money I realised that actually all it is is money. Fundamentally, just spending money is okay; it's rather nice but it gets a bit boring.

Did you feel like you had a purpose then?

I realised that a life without purpose is seriously vacuous. But I had to experience that to know it. When my dad had his accident my mother's goal was always: we've got to make money, we've got to have enough. We didn't have money so she was just always about we've got to have money, and then she was going to retire when she had enough money and then she died.

Are you happy now?

Happier than I've ever been in my life. And that started immediately with OzHarvest. It just came together when I made that decision to start investing in something outside of me. I realised that giving is just so much more than getting. When you experience that, really giving, it's very empowering.

So have you always had that kind of a strong empathy with people?

Yes – I was brought up to have those values. It means I surround myself with the things that bring me joy and don't cause pain to anybody, but make a difference. Surrounding myself with my family, the people I love, the work that is so meaningful for me, and some sacred spaces that I can enjoy, to meditate, to ponder, to think about my life and be grateful in.

And have you designed your life? Have you designed, say, the next three years?

I've designed the rest of my life! It's been a process. I've never been unhappy in any of the phases, but clarity around what I needed for my life has now all come together.

So in the past were you just kind of letting life happen to you?

Yes, I think so. I guess other people would say there was always a direction and I was goal-oriented and that I needed to build up a business, I needed to get financial security, I needed to get my personal fulfilment, and then I needed to find a balance in my life. So those have been the stages.

With this book I want people to understand that it actually is an option, to design your life. Design is not just about choosing bedding, you know, furnishings and things like that!

That's right. You design your life. I love where you're taking the concept.

And then you can actually take control of your life and make it happen, with a proactive approach to mapping out what's going to work with you, and finding out what's best for you, best for your skillset, your natural abilities and things like that.

And for people who feel trapped – you need courage. You do need to believe that you're worthy of this life; you make your life. Some people don't believe they deserve a good life, or they believe they've been given their life and that's what they have to take. And that's not the case. It would be terrible to have a life that you kind of look back at, you know, when you're much older and go, you know, I wish I'd

done this, I wish I'd done that, I got stuck in this job, I didn't really do what I wanted to do...

So many people have come to me over the past nine years and said, one day when I'm either as rich as you or have the time or have paid off all my bills, one day I'm going to do what you've done. I just look at them and say, that's an excuse, it's not a reason.

That one day is never going to happen, is it?

And that's why I say it does take courage to say, actually, I don't want to live another day planning for a day when I might not even be here.

Do you think people don't listen to their intuition?

Yes, I think they've lost the ability to trust that feeling. That's why I say it takes courage. What's the worst that can happen? If it didn't work out quite the way you'd planned it, it doesn't mean that you can't trust that instinct again. There are just so many forces that come into play; I do think we lose the capacity to believe in ourselves.

I wonder when that starts, because we all start out with that potential.

It is complex because you see insecure people, and you have to recognise that it probably comes from when they were little; it comes from deep inside of us. And there are obviously situations where people have genuine problems. Or there are things they can't do.

You enjoy singing, don't you?

I do, I just don't do it very well! I don't let that stop me, though.

Well, I think that you've certainly proved that yes is a powerful word and a powerful attitude towards life, and you've achieved so much with that, and it creates so much positivity not just for yourself but for other people. "Yes" is one simple word, slightly bigger than no, one more letter.

Yes, I love that image; it's a little bit bigger than no but so much more powerful ●

ASPIRE TO INSPIRE

BEFORE YOU EXPIRE

Eugene Bell Jr., Author and entrepreneur

PRINCIPLE 11:   Don't Be the No Man

The No Man is somebody in the habit of repeatedly saying "no". They just say it. They don't even think about it. It's a knee-jerk reaction. It's not a "maybe" or "I'll think about it". It's a firm "no". Saying no is a form of protection. It's hiding from the world rather than stepping into it. It keeps you from connecting with others and experiencing new territories. It's closing doors. It creates a domino effect – saying no doesn't just close one door, it could potentially be closing millions of doors in your lifetime. Just think of that.

M

...SO DON'T SHUT DOWN FIND A GAP IN THE LAYERS OF "NO"

y son Louie had been wearing size 7 shoes. I could see his feet were bursting out of these things. But he wouldn't hear of changing. He loved these shoes but I could see his toenails poking through the fabric. Finally he gave in and we went to the shoe store. They measured his feet. He should have been in a size 10! He was like a Chinese princess with bound feet. ___The next morning he's wearing his new shoes and I'm looking at him and it strikes me: ___"You're taller than me."___"No, he's not." ___That's my other son, Luca. "I am." So we stood there, comparing ourselves, me and these two giants. Now normally mornings are a stressful time in my house. Preparing lunches, getting school kit together, constantly reminding the boys of this and that, me despairing if they'll ever organise themselves. ___But that morning I caught myself in the mirror of life. I was genuinely laughing. Laughing. Un-guarded. I let myself be me. And I wondered, in all these years of being a dad have I been stressed and angry? Is that who they've been seeing all this time? The "no" man? ___Your family are often the ones to suffer the repercussions of a stressful day. How you deal with it really affects them. You are their teacher. You are their coach. It's a precious time. Never forget that. ___So... Don't shut down. Find a gap in the layers of "no". Designers never take "no" for an answer; the very essence of creativity is "What if we could...?" There's always a way. Of course, sometimes you do have to say no, to protect your boundaries, or to stop you getting distracted from the task at hand. But don't get in the habit of just saying "no" without thinking about it. Be thankful for what you have. Open yourself to positivity. See how it is within your power to experience joy and happiness. When you do, you transform yourself ●

The NO man, Louie

DON'T BE THE NO MAN

1 6 0

wha

we co

(if)

uld...

THERE'S ALWAYS A WAY

no
hör

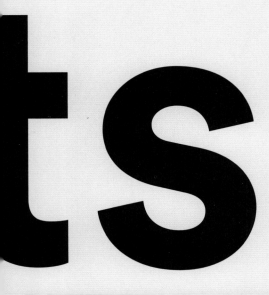

ts

don't say no unless you have to

thr○th

take your time when making a decision

yes is bigger than no

"To avoid criticis

do NOTHING,

, say **NOTHING,**

e **NOTHING."**

Elbert Hubbard, Writer, publisher and philosopher

PRINCIPLE 12: <u>Be Open to Abundance</u>

When you seek out opportunities for connection, when you put yourself on the front line, you create abundance in your life. When you say "yes", you challenge yourself to produce. You have to pace yourself, of course, but by staying open to new possibilities you keep energy flowing through your life.

d comes around w

m around co

s around comes around what

what goes around comes around what goes around comes around what goes around what goes around comes around goes around comes around

NEW OPPORTUNITIES, NEW IDEAS,

Painting 'inspiring ideas to life' on our studio walls

We'd be a smaller company if I were more selective, but I like working at a fast pace, almost frantic. You start to question yourself when you have too much time. The key is to get the ideas out of your head and on to the page. People are pumped and energised by seeing so much work go through the business. It's filled with that entrepreneurial spirit of thinking of new opportunities, new ideas, of digging deep and stretching ability. ___My studio is a potential army of entrepreneurs. The whole studio needs to know how the business works and the role they can play. They have potential connections for new opportunities through friends, family and neighbours. The more they make those connections, the more work we'll have. We're constantly hunting for new work. It means attending events. Going to talks. Giving lectures. Following careers: that marketing director who hired us last year has a new job. Let's reconnect. It's tactical. ___And it's not just material production; abundance also means stating your opinions and following through on commitments. It means adding your voice to the conversation in a clear, considered way. Spreading the buzz, building on what you have and recognising the potential that's sitting at the table around you. Being engaged in the moment, fulfilling your purpose. Abundance is coming from a positive place ●

DIGGING DEEP AND STRETCHING +
A B I L I T Y .

"Periods of t
seldom proli
achievement. M
STIRR

nquillity are

of creative

nkind has to be

UP."

Alfred North Whitehead, Mathematician, logician and philosopher

:-(((((shi

you influence those around you

Wired for the Future

Scott Dadich is the Editor-in-Chief
of *Wired* magazine.

Scott Dadich

INTERVIEW 07:

**Do you believe that new technology is going to
contribute to making us happier and healthier?**
Yes, I do. I think it's important to have an optimistic
view of the future. It may just be that I've been
involved with WIRED for eight years and it has
rubbed off on me, but I think that view might be also
a function of living and working in the Silicon Valley.
People here undertake work because we believe
we're making a difference and that humankind is
making progress and great strides forward. If you
look at the decline in the number of people living in
poverty around the world, the increases in human
literacy, and just basic facets of modern life that
allow for human development, that progress is
hard to deny.

**That's the positive side of technology, but there's
also the problem of feeling saturated. We're accessible 24/7; we don't turn off. What about that side
of things?**
There is definitely a double edge to it. The science
is far from settled, but there's evidence that exposure to technology interferes with the developmen-
tal progress of kids. Some studies have shown that
kids under two shouldn't interact with touchscreens,
because they're at a point where so much of the
brain is developing. We have to be really careful
about it. I struggle with my own addiction to
information and media and connectivity. I was on
vacation with my wife in Hawaii last week, and the
phone was with me the whole time. I got better as
the week went on. I was making a constant effort
to be in the moment or read a book—and leave the
phone in my hotel room—but finding a healthy
balance is something that I don't think we have
a good handle on yet as a society.

**You've also talked about the responsibility
of companies to produce quality information,
because there's so much crap that's being
sent around the world; anyone can say anything
at any time.**
Yes, these days everyone becomes a publisher at
some point, and everyone has global media reach.
And that volume of information is going to increase
exponentially as the next billion and then the next
billion are connected. I don't think we understand
what that's going to look like. I think one of the most
interesting design challenges today is going to be
how we organise and deal with that kind of information overload.

**The digital world is starting to leak into the
physical one. How do you design for that?**
The conventions are only just starting to be under-
stood. The Disney MagicBand is a good example
of where it's going. When you visit Disney World
wearing one of these high-tech wristbands, you
can interact with a layer of digital information

180

The Search for the
Stress Vaccine

#ATTFAIL
Inside the
iPhone Network
Meltdown

╋

**The Deadly
Genius of
Roadside
Bombs**

WIRED

great expectations | aug.2010

WHY
WE
STILL
DON'T
HAVE...

- Laser Guns
- Self-Driving Cars
- Food in a Pill
- Robot Servants
- Vat-Grown Meat
  and more!

with
GUEST
TIME TRAVELER
WILL FERRELL

THE
FUTURE
THAT NEVER HAPPENED
(What We Learn When Technology Flops)

that overlays your physical experience. You're taking your daughter to the park, and when you walk by It's a Small World you can wave your wristband to skip the line and walk on to the ride. And when you're on it, the characters know that your daughter's name is Sally and that it's her ninth birthday. Just below the surface, a lot of design decision-making goes into that experience. But to your daughter it's going to appear like magic—the characters know her name and that it's her birthday, and that's going to be really special for her. Experiences like this—taking place in a kind of hybrid virtual and physical reality—are a new frontier for designers.

What motivates you?
I'm driven by a desire to improve and learn and get better at my craft. I think I've always been motivated by that. Seeing and appreciating the progress you've made can keep you pushing forward. It's hard when you're on the inside, but when you can look back and see how far you've come, that's a really powerful motivation for me. I'm also inspired by my colleagues and by problem-solving. I love having a set of challenges, kicking them around with my team, you know: Is this problem design-related or is there an issue with the storytelling? I get bored quickly when there aren't things to work on. I like doing things for the first time, and I like being on the edge of innovation and being recognised for that. I love being part of the thought leadership, whether that's here in the Valley or in publishing or in media more broadly. I'm also working on being in the moment, and when I get there, that's a really gratifying, empowering place to be.

How did you make the transition from designer to editor? Was that a natural transition for you?
It was, because I was always afforded a seat at the decision-making table, starting with my very first magazine job at *Texas Monthly*. My editor valued my point of view and storytelling aptitude and sense of editorial pacing; making a magazine is a very experience-driven exercise. Think about how one person opens a magazine, goes to the contents, flicks to a particular story. And then think about the person who starts back to front or hops around. There are so many elements that need to be integrated—the visual design and the storytelling and the individual sentences. At *Texas Monthly* I was treated as an equal, not as someone just there to decorate the work of the writers or the editors. I was even called a journalist as a designer; that gave me a great deal of confidence, and I was able to learn a lot in a very safe environment. And that just continued as I worked for Chris Anderson, the previous editor-in-chief of WIRED. That job was equal parts design and storytelling. The best editors are great designers, and the best designers are also great editors.

Do you feel that you have a balance between right-brain and left-brain thinking?
I guess I do, but I don't necessarily see it as an advantage. It's something that I struggle with a bit because I know there are much better designers out there than me. Just like I appreciate and marvel at the craftsmanship of a phenomenal writer, someone who can take the threads of reporting and knit that into compelling prose. I feel like I'm good at a lot of things but not great at any one thing, and sometimes that's uncomfortable for me.

When did you discover your mojo—what worked for you, the thing that you absolutely loved? And was it design?
I don't think it was actually design per se; I loved participating in the design process and how that leads to this thing you've all got in your hands—that app, that poster, or that magazine cover. That's a really charged experience for me. But I guess I define my mojo as understanding that I was that person who could add a little bit to a lot of different processes. I was the guy who could take a B+ and

turn it into an A, whether that was a story or the construction of a headline or the design of a cover or the making of a photograph. I found comfort in a lot of different places in the creative process, and I guess I found some confidence when I let go of this notion that I was only a designer. I have facility in design but I also have facility with language, and I was able to move between those two worlds with some degree of ease.

How do you manage to stay on top of such a demanding role?
I don't know that I'm on top of it, but I can look at it as one task in front of the other, and I have a bit of comfort in the knowledge that I've been in this position before. I've been at this company for eight years and built teams and made progress. It's great to know that the direct application of hard work and thoughtful collaboration with colleagues is going to get me somewhere. I don't know where we're going to end up, but I do know that being deliberate about it and bringing as many decisions together in the right order is possible and it's probably going to get us to a good place. And if we're not in a good place, we'll turn around and try a different path, but that has been a thing that helps me make sense of my day and also the range of decisions that I encounter in any given experience.

What is your mindset when you embark on a new project? Are you optimistic? Or do you like to keep expectations low?
I'm very used to walking out to the edge of the diving board and knowing that there will most likely be water. My experience has taught me to have faith that pretty much every time, yes, something does get made. Sometimes you don't know how deep that water is or even if there's enough to land in. There's this terror that most magazine people encounter: You start with forty blank white pages—no words, no pictures, no designs—and it's going to go to the printer, so you better figure out a way to fill it with amazing stories ●

I'M VERY USED TO WALKING OUT TO THE EDGE OF THE DIVING BOARD AND KNOWING THAT THERE WILL MOST LIKELY BE WATER.

imagine a life without joy

Everyone in the world knows about something in more detail than you do. Making the effort to connect with people is a chance to extract that information and learn new things. On the street, in a coffee shop, on a plane – opportunity is everywhere. Seeing it and taking it is a whole other ball game. As a designer, seeing the opportunity to make things better, smaller, bigger or safer, or more popular, sustainable or profitable, fills my head every second of the day. I believe everyone has the ability to see everyday things as opportunities, rather than seeing things just as they are. That person in the seat next to you? He or she could become a friend for life.

ere!?

14

I've spent _____ hours on a plane without speaking to a soul. A 777 of humanity and what did I do? I pretended they weren't there. I watched television. And at the end, they all got up and walked out of my life. I gave and received no business cards, no names, created no memories. And yet those people are connected with shedloads of other people. I didn't talk to the taxi driver on the drive from the airport, nor the receptionist at the hotel. I was in restaurants teeming with people. Not a single connection with an individual. ___I keep seeing myself on that plane. Yes, I was on a crowded plane, it would have been bizarre to start handing out business cards. "Hey there, designer for hire. Enjoying the flight?" And it's okay to just switch off and enjoy the disconnection with the earth. But how many people on that plane realise the potential opportunities around them? ___ Sometimes, my partner will make me go out in the evening when I think it's the last thing I want to do. I even think about pretending to be asleep to avoid it! But inevitably, once we're out and talking to people, I start having a great time and making connections. That first push out the front door is the hardest. Get past it and the rewards are out there. ___If you give out to the world, you get it back. If you radiate negativity, negative things happen to you. And if you're positive, you find an abundance of positive things come back to you. Opportunities are all around you every second of the day. If you're open to them.

And then the real work begins ●

IF YOU GIVE OUT TO THE WORLD YOU GET IT BACK

Atomic sky on a flight to Johannesburg

"Tomorrow

will be less"

Philippe Starck, Designer

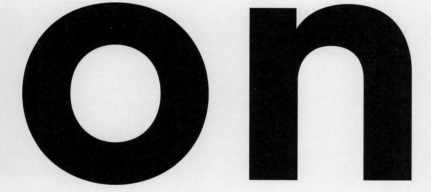

envisage your future but live fully in the now

A Positive Mindset

Justin Hemmes is a property developer
and the CEO of Merivale.

Justin Hemmes

INTERVIEW 08:

What does "design your life" mean to you?
Design shapes everyone's experience, they may not
realise it, but it does. I don't think you can design
your life but I believe that design affects your life.
I know with hospitality, it's the subtleties of design
that really affect whether you enjoy a venue or not.
Obviously, you have to have the fundamentals right,
you have good product and good service, but then
the design around how the environment that you're
eating or drinking in, or how you're being served, or
how you experience that product, which all comes
down to design, really, has a huge effect on your
impression of the space and of your night, or your
afternoon, or your lunch.

In a subconscious way, design is incredibly important. I think design should be subtle and subconscious, not too overpowering and present.

What does it mean to you to be present?
I'm always in the moment; I don't know where else
you could be. The only time I wouldn't be present is
if I'm in a situation where I'd rather be somewhere
else because there's an opportunity that's on my
horizon and I'm thinking about that.

**What does opportunity mean for you and does that
motivate you? Are you an opportunist?**
I certainly am an opportunist, but for me, everything
is an opportunity. It's what you do with it. I would
love to be able to take on every opportunity but
you can only do so much. It's about your perception
of things. One person might think a situation is a
problem whereas another sees an opportunity, it's
how you perceive things and if you're positive then
opportunities arise all the time.

**Do you think they're already there and
people just don't notice them if they're not in
the right frame of mind?**
Of course. When I'm in a positive mindset I see ten
times more opportunities than if I'm not, so, the trick
to it is to try and be in a positive mindset all the time.
Opportunities are also about your imagination and
your level of excitement and your energy level.

**And do you have any advice for people on how
to be alerted to opportunities?**
You need to know your stuff, you need to know your
craft, and then more opportunities arrive because
you have a depth of knowledge about what can be
turned into a positive result. The more attuned you
are to your field or that industry, the more things
you see as opportunities.

And if you believe in yourself and in your product
and what you do, then you're 95 percent of the way
there. I think, if you doubt yourself, then you're less
than 50 percent of the way there.

Aerialists perform at Pacha Sydney, the weekly music event at ivy

Do you use your intuition a lot in business?
Every day. That's my number one research method. Business to me is fun. If I'm going to get enjoyment out of something then most likely I'm going to take it on. If it's not going to be enjoyable, then I don't want to take it on. It has to be, it should be and I'm fortunate enough that it is for me.

You've got a full life; do you separate fun in business and in your personal life, or is it one thing to you?
It's all the same to me. It's a fuzzy line between work and pleasure. I'm doing a new development at the moment and I get so much enjoyment out of it that that is my social life. To go down there at 5.30 in the morning and be on site and see something come to life – I get more excitement from that than any social event or activity, apart from kiteboarding and windsurfing. I'm an avid windsurfer and I've just got into kiteboarding recently and I'm loving it.

To me my business is about pleasure, it's something I love doing and I live and breathe it and it excites me, so it just feels right. So my business has evolved organically just from my enjoyment of the industry and then out of that, the success has followed which allows us to continue to develop the business.

What about designing your future, your wellbeing?
I don't do that; I'm the opposite to that. I just live day to day and live for now and I think by living for now that designs your life. That naturally leads to what should come next. I think if you try and pre-empt your life, it's artificial.

I guess if it wasn't going well you would probably want to redesign your life, wouldn't you?
Yes. I'd work out what I'm not happy about and then change those elements. Because if things aren't going well, you have to be conscious enough to identify what the problem is so you can change it. Obviously financial issues arent easy to change but normally it relates to work, and that comes back to opportunity and doing the things that you love and knowing your craft.

What about for people who get trapped or don't understand that there are opportunities?
You need to be really conscious of your situation, your position and know that everyone is skilled at something or can be skilled at something. You need to find that thing and focus on it.

How did you find yours?
By accident. I was working for my family and hated the job I was doing, so I ran away from home to be a brickies labourer until I decided what I wanted to do. And so I did that by chance, just to fill in time and I fell in love with development. And at the time I was going out and I combined development with going out and having fun and that's how I got into hospitality. All because I had a flip-out one day and out of that came a huge positive, a great opportunity.

So you felt intuitively it wasn't right, what you were previously doing?
Yes. I was doing paperwork for my parents, and I hated it. I was in an office and I didn't enjoy it, it was just a job. And then I went and worked as a brickies labourer and I just loved it, I'd never done it before. I thought I'd do it for six weeks to clear my head and work out what direction I wanted to go in life, and I ended up doing it for two and a half years.

I fell in love with all trades, with bricking, with chippies, with sparkies, with everything, from the joinery work to electrical, membraning, waterproofing, tiling. And then I fell in love with what could go into a physical building, what actually goes into making that space, it's phenomenal, and that intrigued me. And then I fell in love with property and buildings and I just saw them in a different light and it's now my passion. I love architecture and design and thinking about how they fit into the way we live our lives now. To me the most intriguing design challenge is the home because the traditional design of our living spaces doesn't take into account how we actually want to live our lives. And now architecture is starting to think about how the individual wants to live their life and you need to be in tune with that.

It's about designing the right environment for you specifically.
Without a doubt. Residential design should be custom designed around the individual and their preference for how they live, and everybody's different.

It makes a huge difference to your energy, doesn't it, when it's right?
Your whole outlook on life and your perception and your attitude is affected by it. If you go into a space that suits your persona, you feel positive and you have a different outlook on life. It's so important.

And what about your wellbeing, what do you do to look after yourself?
I enjoy life to the extreme, but I actually live a very healthy life. I eat extremely well, I grow my own vegetables, fruit and herbs; I have my own chickens at home and eat their eggs. I eat a lot of organic produce, most of which I grow myself. I certainly believe that what you put into your body is what you get out. There's always a time to indulge but it's a balance. I'm healthy. I exercise, I'm outdoors, I'm in the water all the time, I enjoy looking after myself.

Something that's always struck me is the Australian can-do attitude towards life; do you think that's a generalisation or do you think that's actually true?
Australians traditionally are probably more easy-going, she'll be right mate. But that's changing. I've seen a change over the last 20 years. We've grown out of the tall poppy syndrome and there's a lot more positive outlook and energy. People aspire and look up to success stories now whereas, I think, 20 or 25 years ago, people wanted to hear failures. That tall poppy syndrome is certainly diminishing now, which is a good thing.

What do you think is the key to success in business?
It's not just about business, it's about doing your job well. When I was a labourer and I was given a job to do, say membraning, I did it for six months and I wanted my membrane to be perfect and never leak. I didn't want it to leak for 20 years, so I made sure I did the best job I could possibly do. I'm not trained in it, I'm not a painter, but I learnt how to do it and I made sure I did it as best as that job could be done.

You don't have to have your own business, you don't have to be the boss; it's about being the best at what you do, or at least aspiring to do the job as well as you possibly can do it and not have a "she'll be right mate" mentality. It's a personal thing, no one else saw my membraning. No one goes, "What a great membraning job, that's amazing." It was a personal challenge, I wanted to do a great job and I won't ever do a job that's half-hearted.

Where has that come from?
It came from my dad. If there was a drain blocked, we would clean the drain, we would find out where that drain goes to, we would then open the pit, get down in there and clean the pit out, whether it's full of sand or garbage or shit or whatever it was. It was about doing every job to the greatest of your ability. If something wasn't working at home, you had to clean it or fix it. It would turn into a half-day experience, but that's where it came from.

Did you find it a chore or did you enjoy it?
As a kid I'd say it was a chore. You want to go and hang with your friends, but then it happened so many times it just gets ingrained into your being and that's just how things are now. But I wouldn't swap it for anything. Great teaching.

In a way it's helped you along.
It certainly shapes you, your upbringing. My father had a terrible upbringing yet he had this incredibly positive mindset and can-do attitude. He passed it on to me. I had an amazing upbringing and I have the same attitude as him. He turned his past into a positive, while I had an incredible, wonderful upbringing and I kept that as a positive ●

cha

nge

your life doesn't get better by chance, it gets better by change

PRINCIPLE 14:   Eat the Frog

"Eat the Frog" has become a business axiom. It's the 80:20 principle: 20 percent of the task is hard, 80 percent is closing the deal. If you have to eat a live frog, it doesn't pay to sit around looking at it. Resist the temptation to start with the easier task and do the hardest thing first. Don't waste time, just eat the damned frog. You will be more effective, productive and successful as a result. And, if you have to eat two frogs, eat the ugliest one first.

PROCRAS-TINATION IS TRYING TO HOVER IN A PLACE THAT'S NOT SCARY

have a special form of procrastination: I take on even more work. I'm living life in a state of constant occupation. My normal is hectic. ___I was scheduled to give two talks, London and New York. I got nervous thinking about the talks. How can I do it better? (Perfectionism can be a very effective way of talking yourself out of getting started.) I've given hundreds of talks but somehow I took on a simple challenge and made it insurmountable. I made it a frog. So I went out and found a new house. I found other tasks that would be frogs in their own right. I was frog blinded. ___Procrastination is trying to hover in a place that's not scary. Why would anyone want to do something that's hard? ___I like to vacuum my house. When I am focused on that, I feel good. At one with myself. At peace. It's meditative: I'm back in White Rock stacking shelves at the grocery, every label lined up. If you're going to do it, do it well. But there's more to it. I let it occupy my mind. The roar of the vacuuming sucking up all the crap from the floor and my brain. It's the same with running. When I do my run, I can't do anything else. I'm running. That's my thing. I'm moving and that's all I'm doing. It's a break. A pleasurable avoidance. Am I running or running from frogs? ___If only someone could set me a giant false frog to scare me into action, make me eat all the other frogs and then tell me that there was no frog in the first place. God, life is complicated. ___I realise now that moving to another country was a frog creation exercise. I was avoiding a bigger problem. The biggest: my relationship was terrible. Moving to another country was a way of avoiding that bigger issue. I thought I was buying myself time. But I was robbing myself of time. ___Procrastination is the thief of time. So just get on with it. Eat the frog ●

EAT THE FROG

20²

don
def

'teet

do try to stay focused

"Eat a live fr

in the morning and

WILL HAPP

rest of

g* first thing
NOTHING WORSE
N to you the
e day."

*(sorry frogs and vegetarians)

you can achieve anything with a can-do attitude

n't

Getting Things Done

David Allen is a productivity consultant and the creator of the time management method known as 'Getting Things Done'.

David Allen

INTERVIEW 09:

Is it human nature to procrastinate?
I think the real issue is human fear; the fear of being out of control. People are killing themselves and each other as we speak just to achieve or maintain a sense of psychological control. It's that powerful a driver of our behaviour. Even in more normal and sane circumstances, that still translates. Neither you nor I feel very comfortable in a void. It makes you feel out of control, and that can be physical, mental, physical or emotional. Mentally, out of control translates to: "I'm not sure what to do next, I quit." That's why the "next action" concept of *Getting Things Done* is so powerful because if you haven't figured out your next action yet, there is a part of you that experiences a void in what you've committed to finish. You're not sure what to do so you basically just want to not think about it. If someone says, "Just punch in three numbers, and make them helvetica and red," then hey, you can do that. But I give you a blank and I bet you go, "Ah, out of control." You don't like that feeling. And that conversation you need to have with somebody close to you and you're afraid of how you're going to feel about how they're going to feel when you tell them something you've got to tell them. Those are the kinds of things you'll tend to avoid more than anything.

Do you think today we take on too much?
It's the stress of opportunity. I mean all I have to do is throw you in a crisis, like your house on fire, and you won't have any trouble making decisions or getting highly focused. Get focused on that task and you'll just start to naturally program yourself and take a course of action. That's why crisis gets people highly productive; it produces a lot of constraints which force you into decision making. The reason opportunity is stressful is because of the idea that whatever you produce has to be right or perfect or valuable.

How can people be productive on a regular basis rather than working in fits and starts?
Essentially, you need to get started, you need to start throwing paint on the wall, and then move forward from there. The key is, how do I start to get engaged? As soon as you get going, your creative juices start flowing and you just start to get good ideas and summarise. So it's just jumping through that first hoop. Perfectionism and the fear of being out of control are the two things that will keep you from just stepping in and engaging. How deep is this water? Who cares; jump off. You can swim. Go. Anything that can get you to do that, and can unstick that, those are master keys.

What does "design your life" mean to you?
The strange thing is that the design is already there. There's a part of you that has a sense of whether you're on or off; the design is already pushing or pulling on you. It's not about creating something new; it's really about uncovering the essence.

It's your intuition, isn't it?
Yes. But most people couldn't tell the difference
between intuition and indigestion; they're distracted
by dealing with so much screwed-up stuff just about
the day-to-day of their life. Every one of us has
a still small voice, but it depends on how much noise
is around you. Moving into reflective mode or meditative mode is all about how to quiet one noise so
you can listen to the other messages that are going
on internally.

**How do you deal with being in demand without
diluting the quality of the outcome?**
There's an absolutely foolproof answer to that and
you're involved in it right now. It's called, get older.
You develop the willingness to say you know, that's
not a project I want to take. To think about where
are you going, which things are in alignment to that?
That's your challenge to say, okay, am I willing to
not take the dollar, and not take that client because
that's going to take a bandwith that I need to put
to cooler things and more fun folks to work with.
A fascinating thing is that when you tell people and
you're honest with them, they really get it. And so
they'll tend to appreciate you, and you'll actually
help them by modelling and demonstrating your
own limitations. To be able to make sure you're
doing good work for people that are expecting it
of you.

What motivates you?
I can't stop doing good work for people doing good
work, and I want to help them, I want to improve
conditions. I'm connected to people and people
come to me in a positive, open context and want the
systems so if I have something that could improve
their lives, wow, how could I not do that?

Have you designed your life?
No, not really. But I've done visualisation techniques;
I did one back in 1991; I haven't done one since
because I'm living out that thing I drew. I had colour
pens and I just drew this little map of what my ideal
life would be like, including being connected with
the world through some sort of electronic media that
would allow me to spread my work in some higher
leverage way, and I'm actually living that life now.

YOUR MIND IS FOR HAVING IDEAS, NOT HOLDING THEM

I'm a firm believer that whatever images you hold in your mind will affect your perception and your performance and are going to automatically move you in those directions. At the end of every year, my wife and I do an acknowledgement exercise; we make a list: this cat died, or this was the first time we went to Norway and looked at the northern lights. Or we hired this person or we changed this thing about our business. Then we take the next twenty minutes to say what would we like to have on that list at the end of next year.

Did you have times in your life where you had problems getting things done?

I've always been interested in how I can get things done more easily. That can take a lot of different forms, from which way should I walk out of this room that would take the fewest steps, all the way to what's my life purpose and what's the best way to make that happen? So all of those are about efficiency. I've always been driven, in a sense, out of my laziness. How do I maximise what I'm doing? I will only organise to the degree to which it makes it the easiest way to get things done. Not to just get organised.

I've always been interested in models. How does applying a model change and improve things? I didn't get any smarter or work any harder, I applied a model. Here's a way to think about how to write a proposal. Here's a way to think about how I approach this next design. And so on. What's the model that gets something off your mind without having to finish it there and then? You don't have to transform yourself, you just supply something that makes things work better. Just pure efficiency.

And the best way to get things done is tell yourself, go clean the toilet. Give yourself some awful thing to do that you feel like you have to do and I guarantee you, you will get all your other design projects finished in time.

How would you recommend the average person get proactively engaged in being the best they can be?

I think the key is for people to recognise: when should you and your staff get together and think and at what horizon? Where do we want to be three years from now? Or whatever. Many times this conversation will be driven by circumstances so people think at these different horizons because the world forces them to. Often, people wait until their company suddenly got divested or bought or they just got fired or they just found out they've got a life-threatening illness or whatever. Often those are the times that people are forced to think at different levels. The more you can start to pay attention to what horizon right now would be useful for us to think about and to look at, that then might inform some of our decisions of what we do or don't do right now. It's a process question that you constantly ask yourself in order to stay fresh, current, healthy; as best you can in what you're doing.

How do you balance getting things done with relaxing, spending time with your family, staying healthy and all that important stuff?

Well, here's the secret. Getting things done is not about getting things done. It's about getting yourself appropriately engaged with your life. Are you appropriately engaged with your health? Are you appropriately engaged with your family? Are you appropriately engaged with that project for that client? Are you appropriately engaged with your cat?

It's all about being able to quiet yourself so you can be fully present with whatever you're doing. The people I know who are most truly adept at being or doing are the ones who've figured out whatever they can't *not* do. Whenever time disappears, whenever you get into your zone, that's actually being. When you're into your zone and you go, oh lunch time, what happened, where did the morning go? Whatever you were doing, there was no distinction in your mind between personal or professional; there was no concern about time. That should be the normal as opposed to the exceptional event.

How do you deal with not being able to give people as much time as they want from you?
You need to make sure that you're managing your agreements with yourself and how you are engaged with this world. At some point, you may go, look, I've got limited time and they're asking an infinite amount of time. I'm doing exactly as much as I can do. You don't have to fulfil everybody's expectations of you. You just need to get comfortable with your own agreements with yourself about how you are engaged with them.

They deal with that. That's not your accountability. That's theirs. If they can't accept you in terms of who you are and what you're about and what your parameters are, they're not the people to play with. They'll learn.

And when it comes to email, just deal with it like you deal with your physical garbage. Having 300 emails in your inbox – that'll teach you to make some decisions pretty fast. All it does is make very evident what's important to you and what's not. You get 50,000 thoughts a day. 300 emails is nothing. I'm not sitting there wondering about the things I'm missing out on. I've got enough to deal with.

Do you think people avoid clear space? Is it an uncomfortable place?
Oh, very uncomfortable. So unfamiliar. Unfamiliar equals uncomfortable. You know, how long can you be happy before some part of you says, oh my god, I should worry about something? You're uncomfortable with a certain span of happiness.

What's your last word in terms of advice on just getting things done for the average person?
The optimal state to be in is clear space in your psyche, in your head. And the only way you get there is to be appropriately engaged with all the aspects of your life and that doesn't mean you have to finish everything; it does mean that you need to decide what it is and where it is and where it goes and review it regularly and that's not easy. That's a great task. But if you're going to play in the world of infinite opportunity and not have it stress you out, that's a requirement ●

ESSENTIALLY, YOU NEED TO GET STARTED, YOU NEED TO START THROWING PAINT ON THE WALL, AND THEN MOVE FORWARD FROM THERE.

you won't know until you give it a go

ust

In my early days as a designer, my intuition was the most valuable tool in my belt. Often my first idea was my best idea and I instinctively knew it. Instant clarity. Selling it to the client with the line "Trust me, it just feels right" was a legitimate approach. Nowadays that won't wash. There needs to be a science behind every decision. But sometimes a great idea just takes a second. Counter to my advice about mentors (looking for people around you) and collaborating, looking inwards is also valuable. Your inner self is giving you answers all the time but it's unquantifiable and most people think it's a load of hokey crap. But it is exactly that intuition – built upon universal experiences and human truths – that determines whether a design is relevant or not. You are unique, so don't listen to me, listen to you.

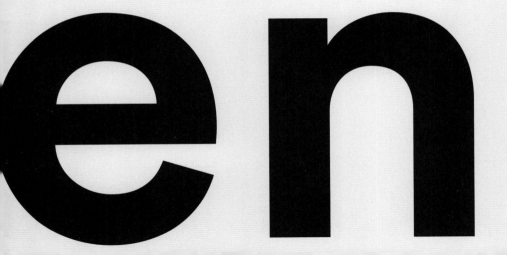

217

DESIGN YOUR LIFE

THE
INTUITIVE
MIND IS
A SACRED
GIFT

AND THE
RATIONAL
MIND
IS A
FAITHFUL
SERVANT

WE HAVE CREATED A SOCIETY THAT HONOURS THE SERVANT AND HAS FORGOTTEN THE GIFT

Popular saying

We arrive in the world fully formed. Not only that, we've been programmed. For what is a spirit, a will, a consciousness other than a biochemical code? It's built into us. That's the nature of nature. Nurture is a trickier proposition: it relies on our environments, engagement with others and ultimately on feedback from ourselves. Nurture is constant reprogramming. So your inner voice is your genes and years of world experience – nature and nurture – talking. ___In life, we can move away from our selves. Our core. We become disconnected and, without intervention, drift further and further away. This is what leads to burn-out, to repeat mistakes, to feelings of failure, inadequacy and fraudulence. We're not listening to ourselves. Worse, we've lost the ability. ___Somewhere I'm still the kid from White Rock with thirteen spleens who fell behind at school. The kid who didn't speak at birthday parties. But there's an advantage to being this kid. It's made me a good listener. To my inner voice, as well as the voices of others. It turns out that not saying anything, just looking around and taking things in, was and still is a very important part of my life. And that's what makes me good at what I do. Listening to the client, walking around in their shoes, seeing the opportunity, and then, hopefully, finding a solution in my gut. And often it comes in a flash. Intuition. A lightning bolt created by every experience and every aspect of my forty-nine years that exists in my head coming together for that split second. ___"I operate very strongly with my instincts. If I don't get it in the first crack, I get it in the second. And if I don't get it in the second, I almost never get it. Design is a very intuitive process for me. I've never been a refiner." Paula Scher, Designer. ___The impulse to design my life was evolutionary. A gradual dawning. If intuition is a valuable design tool, why not an invaluable life tool? Perhaps my evolution began when I started listening to myself. ___Get away from noise and distractions and restore your sense of what feels right and what doesn't.

Find your centre ●

"When you mak
how do you jus
Do you wrap
industry jargon?
an elaborate post-ra
I've done both whe
to express my

Now science is cor
known all along—our
whether a design

a design choice,
fy it to others?
 in a layer of
Do you construct
onalisation? I admit
I've been at a loss
INTUITION.
irming what we've
ntuition determines
s relevant or not."

R Michael Hendrix, Partner at IDEO

trust your senses – they don't lie

Control and Compromise

Paula Scher is a graphic designer and
partner at Pentagram New York.

Paula Scher

INTERVIEW 10:

How much of your design process is driven by intuition?

I'm tremendously driven by intuition. I think most people are, they just aren't aware of it. You make lists and you do research but you intuitively know the answer. I always find that research ends up being a proof of something I intuited just by hearing the problem. You already know the research because you've heard it in other forms, so your intuition isn't something that's coming out of the wind, it's coming out of a lifetime of observation.

Do you apply intuition to your personal life?

In my personal life, I'm very good at using intuition (or that form of reasoning) for things like purchasing real estate, but I don't think it has anything to do with relationships. I think relationships are totally mysterious and any kind of planning or analysis is not in my capacity. That's the nature of relationships, if you try too hard to manage them, you lose the mystery, so I can't say I'm a person who's been very good at designing my life that way. But there are areas where design principles do work in relationships. For example, if you're dealing with day-to-day annoyances with a partner – if you're repeatedly frustrated by something and you try to make them change, you're not likely to because they would have changed already. What you have to do is design a way around it, so you're not irritated by it any more.

What about designing your wellbeing?

That stuff I think you can design. I've balanced my painting with my design work and I've set up a studio and a time schedule and I have to maintain it because I need both things to feel good. At first, it was a way of channelling the loneliness I felt during the long winters in our country house – it was a choice; I took something that was negative and turned it into a positive.

Do you feel that you've designed your life or do you feel that it's just happened to you?

No, I feel like a total victim! (Roars with laughter). I feel like I've muddled and blown and screwed up everything. The only thing I feel I do well is my work – my personal life is a complete mess. Work is sometimes the most enjoyable part of life because it can be pure problem solving and the emotional aspect is taken out of it. That's why it's so satisfying. Obviously it can be exasperating with clients and deadlines, but it's a way of participating and being involved without the emotional stress that can come in a personal relationship.

Do you think the design process has changed in the last decade?

Yes, it's become far more collaborative, but the question is: what is the result? When you have teams of people who are collaborating, it means that they're going to correct each other's mistakes and that's good and bad. What's good about it is you don't have as many mistakes; what's bad is that you homogenise the work and it doesn't become memorable. The reason that Apple has such a strong ability to succeed as a brand is largely because it was one person's vision. When you have multitudes attached to a vision, it weakens.

224

Do your clients ever want you to justify your work with facts or data?

Sometimes they ask for some metrics but you can't do that. For example if you take the theatre, you can promote the play and you can determine how many people went to see it, possibly based on the promotion, but often it's more about the weather. You can't always rate the identity because identity doesn't work like that; it's a cumulative effect over time. It's just not the same as the direct correlation between someone watching a TV ad and buying that product, and even then the information can be misleading. What I like doing is packaging-focused tests, where the better design wins – that's the closest you can get to quantifying the success of an identity.

Do you feel an obligation to design a better world?

I do. I work with the City of New York and a lot of things I've done have improved life here and I'm really proud of that. I've also donated a lot of it and I do it because I live here and I understand it. I don't feel I can fix water in India because I just don't have that capability, but I do feel I have an obligation to raise the expectation of what something can be. If I design something, I want to try and elevate an area, to make it better than the norm. I think that's the goal of design.

What do the words "Design Your Life" mean to you?

It means picking out really good bedroom furniture! (Laughs.) I don't think you can design your life. I think you can make choices, but I'm the person who didn't get to have children and I still don't know why, so you can't talk to me about designing my life because I would have done a better job. But in my work I've made very careful decisions. I know that every five years or so I have to make a major change in the way I approach things or I'm dead. That's the secret to having worked for forty years – you can't stand still, you have to grow. I'm trying to figure out how to be relevant at the age of sixty-five and that's a scary thing. Design is planning and if you want all your plans to come to fruition, it's very disappointing when they don't. So I think you can design your life to a degree but you can't predict the future and you have to be prepared to compromise ●

I CAN'T SAY I'M A PERSON WHO'S BEEN VERY GOOD AT DESIGNING MY LIFE.

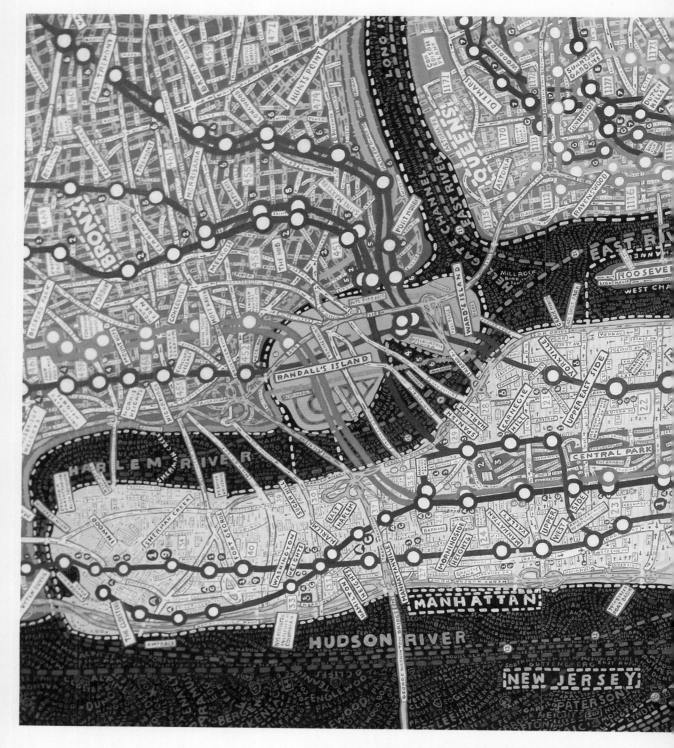

A LOT OF THINGS I H
LIFE HERE AND I AM

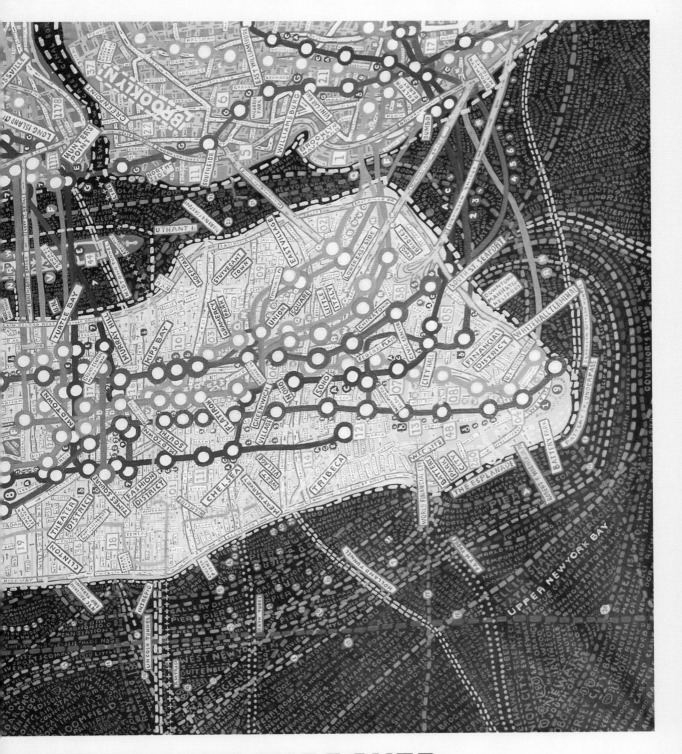

VE DONE HAVE IMPROVED
EALLY PROUD OF THAT.

NYC Transit 2007, Paula Scher

tru
you
intu

emphasise the you in decision-making

st

r

tion

It's <u>NEV</u>
late to I
you mig
be

VER too
be what
ht have
en!

Popular saying

Designing Success

I hadn't seen a work colleague in some time. After working together one morning, we sat down for lunch.

ME:
This is a good salad.

FRIEND:
It is, isn't it.

FRIEND:
You know, Vince, it's an amazing transformation.

ME:
What is?

FRIEND:
You. You're clear. You're level-headed. You're relaxed.

ME:
Really?

ME:
How bad was I?

FRIEND:
You were very abrupt. You had no time for anybody and you were very stressed-out. It's fantastic to see how you have redesigned the way you are.

IT WAS VALIDATING.

The hard work is paying off. I am a more positive person, a more reasonable person. Cutting out alcohol and caffeine, getting lots of exercise, sleeping well, keeping focused, doing everything I do to the best of my ability not just at the office but in the house, on the street, in the shops. Now I have to prove this isn't a temporary state, that this is not the eye in the storm of Hurricane Vince.

That's human nature: we look to the future and worry that we won't succeed. We look at the future, that great intangible promised land that is entirely abstract and we hope, "One day it will all be sorted out." We're eight minutes from the end of everything. If the sun goes nova, that's how long we'll have to ponder.

No, everything will not be sorted out. Life is constantly teaching us, and we're constantly learning, our genes are learning. But I don't feel frustrated and dissatisfied with everything not being right. I stop and look back at my life, my family, the distance I've come. So what if I relapse? So what if I lose my confidence, feel all the brave feelings draining away?

Designing your life isn't about certainty. Designing your life isn't about permanence. It's about incremental change for the better, even with the odd relapse.

Touch the puck five times.

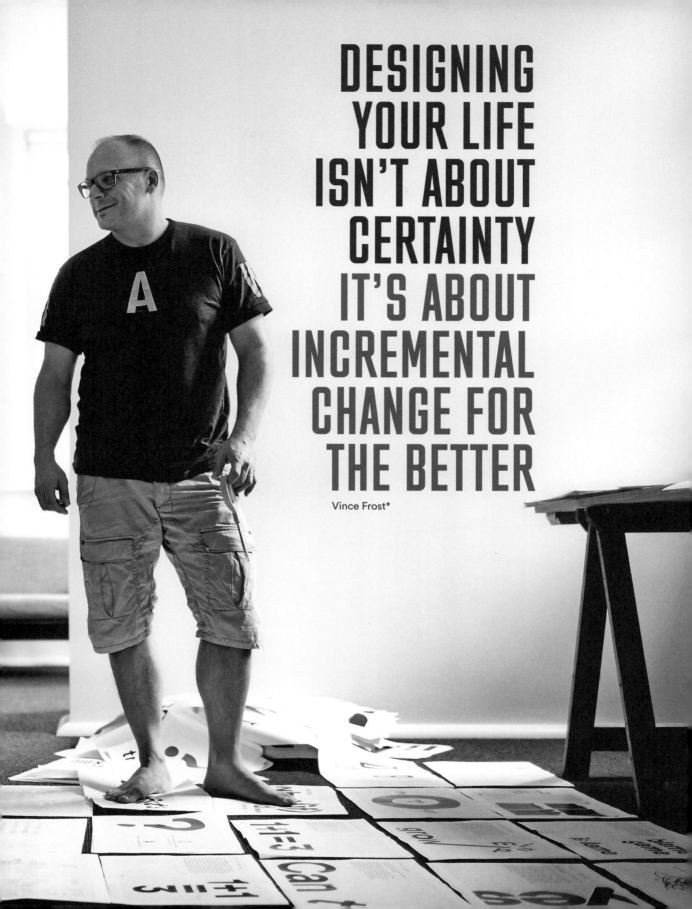

DESIGNING
YOUR LIFE
ISN'T ABOUT
CERTAINTY
IT'S ABOUT
INCREMENTAL
CHANGE FOR
THE BETTER

Vince Frost*

INDEX:

Gia's instant hairdo, Bramber, 2013

CREDITS:

I want to thank everyone who has contributed to the journey of my life so far. Each one of you has influenced me in a positive way and helped me grow. This book took a lot of effort; I couldn't have done it without the support of my team and family. It put everything I talk about in the book to the test.

Miya Bradley You produced this book with relentless optimism and dedication. I've dreamt about being in a relationship like ours and six years ago it came to reality. There is not a day that goes by that I don't think how lucky I am to be a part of your life. You are relentlessly positive both in business and our relationship and I thank you for that.

My Family My questioning beautiful kids, Luca, Louie and Gia, and my inspiring parents, Alan and Irene.

Denis Seguin I enjoyed our rambling Skype conversations each morning and your help in putting my thoughts into meaningful words.

Adam Vella Thank you for your assistance, perseverance and positive attitude. We must have tried a hundred covers and dozens and fonts and grids until the book found its look.

Julie Gibbs Thank you for coming to my Apple store *Design Your Life* talk four years ago and suggesting it become a book. And thank you to the friendly and efficient team at Penguin Lantern: Katrina, Jocelyn, Daniel, Emily and Josette.

My amazing team at Frost* particularly Camilla Belton, Angela Florio, Alissa Prcevich and Helen Prebble. Ant Geernaert for your skill with a camera and documenting the process, and my lawyer Adam Simpson.

Vince Frost would like to thank the following people for their time and assistance with interviews.

Ewan Jaspan (Page 38–41) – Australia's highest-ranking kiteboarder, www.vimeo.com/ewanjaspan

Natalie Slessor (Page 86–87) – Environmental Psychologist, Head of Workplace at Lend Lease

Gabriela Rosa (Page 98–99) – Clinician, author and internationally recognized naturopath and fertility specialist, www.NaturalFertilityHealthSolutions.com

Chris Sanderson (Page 112–115) – Co-founder and CEO of The Future Laboratory, www.thefuturelaboratory.com
Mark Brakspear, Executive Assistant to CEO and Editor-in-Chief

Roy Green (Page 126–129) – Dean of UTS Business School at the University of Technology Sydney, Australia, www.uts.edu.au
Leonie Bringolf, Executive Assistant to Professor Roy Green

Ronni Kahn (Page 152–155) – Social entrepreneur and founder of the food rescue charity OzHarvest, www.ozharvest.org
Marla Minow, Executive Assistant to the CEO

Scott Dadich (Page 180–183) – Editor in Chief of *Wired* magazine, www.wired.com / Blanca Myers, Associate to the Editor in Chief and the team at *Wired*

Justin Hemmes (Page 194–197) – property developer and CEO of Merivale, www.merivale.com
Rebecca Biggs, Publicity Manager, Merivale

David Allen (Page 210–213) – productivity consultant and the creator of the time management method 'Getting Things Done', www.gettingthingsdone.com / Kathryn Allen

Paula Scher (Page 219–227) – graphic designer and partner at Pentagram New York, www.pentagram.com
Sarah Dobson, Project Manager for Paula Scher

Every effort has been made to contact all copyright owners prior to publication of Design Your Life, *to ensure that their contribution is properly acknowledged. Where we have been unable, despite our best endeavours, to make contact we would welcome hearing from anyone concerned, so that we may include an appropriate acknowledgement in any reprints.*

Page 2–3: Quote from *Design for the Real World* by Victor Papanek © 1984 Victor Papanek. Thanks to the Papanek Foundation. Reprinted by kind permission of Thames & Hudson Ltd., London **Page 19:** *Hooligan* by Alan Fletcher and quote by Alan Fletcher reproduced with the kind permission of Paola and Raffaella Fletcher, www.alanfletcherarchive.com **Page 21:** Eames Chaise lounge designed by Charles and Ray Eames. Herman Miller Eames Chaise image courtesy of Herman Miller Inc. www.hermanmiller. com **Page 30–31:** Quote by Paula Scher reproduced with the kind permission of Paula Scher **Page 31:** *Hand Made*, photograph by Giles Revell, www.gilesrevell.com for the cover of Wallpaper* Custom Cover magazine August 2012, www.wallpaper.com **Page 33:** Quote by Michael Gerber reproduced with the kind permission of Michael Gerber, www.michaelgerbercompanies.com **Page 34–35:** Quote by Stefan Sagmeister reproduced with the kind permission of Stefan Sagmeister, www.sagmeisterwalsh.com **Page 38:** Ewan Jaspan interview: Portrait photographer Arterium, www.arterium.net / in the air PKRA event photographer Toby Bromwich, www.tobybromwich.blogspot.com.au **Page 52:** Quote by Richard Branson reproduced with the kind permission of Richard Branson. **Page 68–69:** Quote by Tom Dixon reproduced with the kind permission of Tom Dixon, www.tomdixon.net **Page 82:** Quote by Megan Morton reproduced with the kind permission of Megan Morton, www.meganmorton.com **Page 82–83:** *Painting Box #3* by Mark Collis reproduced with the kind permission of Mark Collis **Page 107:** Quote by Edward de Bono from *Think Before It's Too Late* © IP Development Corporation 2009, Edward de Bono asserts his moral right to be known as the author of this work. Reproduced with the kind permission of de Bono Global, www.debono.com **Page 113:** Image reproduced with the kind permission of The Future Laboratory, www.thefuturelaboratory.com **Page 120:** Quote by Susan Cain reproduced with the kind permission of Susan Cain, www.thepowerofintroverts.com **Page 127:** Model of Dr Chau Chak Wing Building by Gehry Partners LLP. Courtesy of University of Technology, Sydney and Anna Zhu Photography & Film **Page 140–141:** Quote by Bruce Mau reproduced with the kind permission of Bruce Mau, www.brucemaudesign.com **Page 146:** Photograph of wooden hand by Antony Geernaert, www.anthonygeernaert.com **Page 153:** *OzHarvest Annual Report* designed by Frost* Design, photograph by Anthony Geernaert, www.anthonygeernaert.com **Page 156:** Quote by Eugene Bell Jr reproduced with the kind permission of Eugene Bell Jr. **Page 174–175:** Photograph of *Inspiring Ideas to Life* by Ian Haigh, www.ketchup.net.au **Page 176:** Quote from *Dialogues of Alfred North Whitehead* by Alfred North Whitehead, Edited by Lucien Price, Reprinted by permission of David R. Godine, Publisher, Inc. Copyright © 1954 by Alfred North Whitehead, and thanks to the Centre for Process Studies Claremont California USA **Page 180:** Scott Dadich portrait by Planton, www.plantonphoto. com **Page 181:** *Wired* magazine cover August 2010, photograph by Dan Winters, www.danwintersphoto.com. Cover reproduced with the kind permission of *Wired* and Forefront Media. **Page 190:** Quote by Philippe Starck reproduced with the kind permission of Starck Network, www.starck.com. **Page 195:** Image by Pacha Sydney supplied courtesy of Merivale and Pacha Sydney, www.pachasydney.com **Page 220–221:** Quote by R Michael Hendrix reproduced with the kind permission of R Michael Hendrix **Page 224:** Paula Scher portrait by Alisa Connan, www.alisaconnan. com **Page 226–227:** *NYC Transit*, 2007 by Paula Scher, www.paulaschermaps.com **Page 238–239:** Photograph by Anthony Geernaert, www.anthonygeernaert.com

LANTERN:

Published by the Penguin Group
Penguin Group (Australia)
707 Collins Street, Melbourne, Victoria 3008, Australia
(a division of Penguin Australia Pty Ltd)
Penguin Group (USA) Inc.
375 Hudson Street, New York, New York 10014, USA
Penguin Group (Canada)
90 Eglinton Avenue East, Suite 700, Toronto, Canada ON M4P 2Y3
(a division of Penguin Canada Books Inc.)
Penguin Books Ltd
80 Strand, London WC2R 0RL England
Penguin Ireland
25 St Stephen's Green, Dublin 2, Ireland
(a division of Penguin Books Ltd)
Penguin Books India Pvt Ltd
11 Community Centre, Panchsheel Park, New Delhi – 110 017, India
Penguin Group (NZ)
67 Apollo Drive, Rosedale, Auckland 0632, New Zealand
(a division of Penguin New Zealand Pty Ltd)
Penguin Books (South Africa) (Pty) Ltd,
Rosebank Office Park, Block D, 181 Jan Smuts Avenue, Parktown
North, Johannesburg, 2196, South Africa
Penguin (Beijing) Ltd
7F, Tower B, Jiaming Center, 27 East Third Ring Road North,
Chaoyang District, Beijing 100020, China

Penguin Books Ltd, Registered Offices:
80 Strand, London, WC2R 0RL, England
First published by Penguin Group (Australia), 2014

10 9 8 7 6 5 4 3 2 1

Cover, design and illustrations by Vince Frost

Typeset in Circular and MFred. MFred typeface is part of Buy Fonts
Save Lives project. All profits go to Macmillan Cancer Support
and Cancer Research UK, http://typespec.co.uk/mfred-font

Colour separation by Splitting Image Colour Studio,
Clayton, Victoria
Printed and bound in China by C & C Offset Printing Co Ltd

National Library of Australia
Frost, Vince, author.
Design Your Life ®/Vince Frost.
9781921383878 (hardback)
Self-actualisation (Psychology)
Self-help techniques
Life skills.
158.1

penguin.com.au/lantern

LANTERN

"We make a living by what we get, we make a life by what we GIVE."

Popular saying

YOU
CAN